741.43 SCO

£2.50

Martin Scorsese

D0755108

SRC Bede Sixth Form
Marsh House Avenue
BILLINGHAM
Stockton on Tees
TS23 3HB

BEDE SIXTH FORM
B000648

Other titles in this series by the same author

Alfred Hitchcock
Film Noir
Noir Fiction
Orson Welles
Stanley Kubrick
Woody Allen
Hong Kong's Heroic Bloodshed (Editor)

Martin Scorsese

Paul Duncan

SRC Bede Sixth Form
Marsh House Avenue
BILLINGHAM
Stockton on Tees
TS23 3HB

www.pocketessentials.com

This edition published in July 2004 by Pocket Essentials,
P. O. Box 394, Harpenden, Herts, AL5 1JX
http://www.pocketessentials.com

© Paul Duncan 2004

The right of Paul Duncan to be identified as author of this work
has been asserted by him in accordance with the Copyright, Designs &
Patents Act 1988.

All rights reserved. No part of this book may be reproduced, stored in or
introduced into a retrieval system, or transmitted, in any form or by any
means (electronic, mechanical, photocopying, recording or otherwise)
without the written permission of the publishers.
Any person who does any unauthorised act in relation to this publication
may be liable to criminal prosecution and civil claims for damages.

A CIP catalogue record for this book is available from the British
Library.

ISBN: 1 903047 66 8

2 4 6 8 10 9 7 5 3 1

Typography by Avocet Typeset, Chilton, Aylesbury, Bucks
Printed and bound in Great Britain by Cox & Wyman, Reading, Berks

for Claude and Josef

"Twenty dollars! Let's go da movies!"
Charlie, *Mean Streets* (1973)

Acknowledgements

Thanks go to Ellen, Mitch & Colin, John, Ray and Chris for supplying me with more videos, books and articles than I know what to do with, to Ion, Claire and Floss for their support over the past four years, and to Claude and Josef for being there when I finish roaming these mean streets.

Contents

Martin Scorsese: Body and Soul   11

1   Novice   27

2   Doing The Right Thing   49

3   Out On A Limb   85

4   King Of The Kinematograph   117

Reference Materials   153

Martin Scorsese: Body and Soul

"All this filming, it's not healthy."
Peeping Tom (1960)

In Michael Powell's disturbing film *Peeping Tom* (1960), Carl roams the sleazy side of the movie world and films the look of fear on women's faces as he kills them. He uses the camera as a weapon to violate the characters. Carl is just one of many driven or obsessed people at the core of Michael Powell's films. The perfectionism of Lermontov in *The Red Shoes* (1948) leads to the death of the central character. When the ballerina is asked why she dances, she replies, "Because I must." It is no wonder then that Martin Scorsese, whose films concentrate on driven characters, often cites Michael Powell as his favourite director.

Consistently in Scorsese's film, the central character is driven by the pressures and needs of his environment and his inner nature, and these are in conflict with the inner truth that the character is trying to attain. This is an age-old story – how can a sinner be redeemed, be cleansed of their sins, be forgiven in an unforgiving world? As can be seen in *Taxi Driver* (1976, Travis Bickle goes mad, kills lots of bad guys and is hailed as a hero), *Raging Bull* (1980, Jake La Motta is a violent man both inside and outside the ring) and *GoodFellas* (1990, Henry Hill is seduced by the lifestyle of the neighbourhood gangsters), these conflicts are often expressed as bloody fables of modern New York. However, whether consciously or unconsciously, this theme is echoed in many of Scorsese's other films. *Kundun* (1998) shows the eponymous central character holding onto his spiritual purity despite the carnage that is being wrought around him. This is in contrast to *Mean Streets* (1973) where Charlie tries to hold onto his epileptic lover and his psychotic friend in direct violation of the orders of his mob bosses. Similarly, in *The Age Of Innocence* (1993) Newland Archer is obsessed by his love for Ellen Olenska, but he is not brave enough to live outside the etiquette of the times. In contrast, *The Colour Of Money* (1986) shows Fast Eddie Felson finding the courage to pick up a cue again after many years of fear.

In many ways, Scorsese's central characters conform to the definition of the tragic hero laid out by the philosopher Aristotle in one of the earliest known books of literary criticism, *Poetics*. According to Aristotle, the tragic hero is a mixture of good and bad but he is someone people can relate to. If the people were put into the tragic hero's position, they would probably do the same things as the hero does. He has a tragic flaw that is the cause of his downfall and there is a person or thing that sets the stage for his fall. The tragic hero goes on a physical or psychological journey and he always falls at the end. His flaw always results in tragedy for himself and for those around him.

Furthermore, Aristotle formulated three crucial effects of drama: first, the audience develops an emotional attachment to the tragic hero; second, the audience fears what may befall the hero; and finally (after tragedy strikes) the audience pities the suffering hero. In this way the audience experiences a catharsis, their emotions are released. More than anything else, it is this expression and release of emotion that characterises Scorsese's work in a way that links him to his mentor John Cassavetes. Certainly there are intense emotional moments, for example between Jake La Motta and his brother in *Raging Bull*, that evoke the edginess and volatility of the best of Cassavetes' work.

A closer look at Scorsese's characters and stories shows that many of them exhibit the criteria needed to fit Aristotle's definitions. His characters may be more bad than good, and some of them are monsters, but they retain a certain humanity that the audience can hold onto. Witness Vietnam veteran Travis Bickle's vitriolic discourse on the scum of society as he prowls the streets of New York in his taxi. We agree with him because we, too, are afraid of and disgusted by the city at night. We understand this position and so go along with the character. Outside of his taxi and his army clothes – his armour – when Travis tries to pick up prim and proper Cybill Shepherd, he is awkward and tense, but at the same time he has a directness that Shepherd likes. It is only when he takes her to a pornographic movie on their first date that we understand just how different their worlds are, and also that we have given ourselves over to somebody who may not be quite right in the head. We gradually come to realise that this nightmarish vision of New York comes from Travis' mind.

Travis is very angry. He fought in Vietnam for a better America, and America does not seem to have improved in any way. He is without a family, so his quest to seduce Betsy away from the politician Palantine and to save child prostitute Iris from her pimp Matthew could be construed as his desire to be part of normal society by having a family. His rejection by Betsy leads him to attempt an assassination on Palantine (killing the 'father' so 'freeing' Betsy), and when that fails he kills Matthew in the process of rescuing Iris (again killing the 'father' to 'free' Iris).

At the end, Travis is feted as a hero in the press, thanked by Iris' parents in a letter, and he meets with Betsy. This follows the normal conventions of a heroic movie, but with the flash of Travis' red eyes in the rear view mirror, Scorsese is showing us that Travis is still in hell, in the abyss of his mind, and that he has not been redeemed. His moral crusade against the outrages of the world has not finished. In his own eyes he has failed, but he will not stop.

Travis is trapped in his cab, writing about his experiences, disgusted by the world, feeling superior to it and apart from it yet at the same time wanting to be part of it. He displays all the classic symptoms of being an immobilised man, as writer Charles Willeford coined it, a man who is psychologically impotent in the face of modern society. As such, director Martin Scorsese and writer Paul Schrader are continuing a long line of noir fiction that stretches back from Fyodor Dostoyevsky's *Notes From Underground* (1864) – which Scorsese wants to film – to Knut Hamsun's *Hunger* (1890), Joseph Conrad's *Heart Of Darkness* (1899), Jim Thompson's *Pop 1280* (1964) and Charles Willeford's *The Burnt Orange Heresy* (1971). And similarly, they continue the Film Noir tradition but reinterpret it in a psychologically more disturbing manner. (For more information, see my Pocket Essentials on *Noir Fiction* and *Film Noir*.)

However, Scorsese brings two distinctive elements to his films: the environment he grew up in, where the only career choices in his neighbourhood were the priesthood or organised crime; and his love, enthusiasm and knowledge of film. The first element shapes the content of his films and the second shapes their form.

Born 17 November 1942 in Flushing Long Island, Martin Scorsese grew up in Elizabeth Street on the Lower East Side of Manhattan. It was a mixture of Italians, Irish and Jews. His parents, Charles and Catherine, were the children of Sicilian immigrants. They had a strong work ethic and had to struggle to survive. Even though Charles worked all the hours he could in the garment industry, there was never enough money so, to earn extra, he lit gas stoves for Jews on the Sabbath. Scorsese's society had their own rules and regulations – they lived outside of normal society and were not affected by either the law of Washington DC or the police who were there to enforce those laws. For Scorsese and his contemporaries growing up in Little Italy there were only two career options, the mob or the church, both of which had their own conflicting codes of honour and ethics. Scorsese's father would explain these and other rules to his youngest son (Scorsese had an older brother called Frank), and had rules for everything, including the proper way to serve meals.

You can see this environment in Scorsese's most autobiographical films *Who's That Knocking At My Door?* (1968)

and *Mean Streets*. One gets the sense that JR and Charlie's emotional and ethical conflicts are ones that Scorsese lived through and worried about. He continued to use violent New York settings for *Taxi Driver*, *Raging Bull*, *After Hours* (1985), *GoodFellas*, *Bringing Out The Dead* (1999) and *Gangs Of New York* (2002), but it can be argued that all the societies that Scorsese presents in his films, whether it is the etiquette of *The Age Of Innocence*, or the pool hall hustling of *The Colour Of Money*, or the rituals of *Kundun*, all have rules that the characters follow or break at their peril.

The characters must either accept the society they are trapped in or escape it. There is never any hint that his characters can change that society – the society is stronger than any single person. This is most pointedly expressed in *Gangs Of New York* where the climatic fight between Bill the Butcher and Amsterdam Vallon is rendered insignificant when seen in the context of the Draft Riots that overtook New York.

As a child Scorsese had asthma, so was often taken to the cinema because his parents did not know what else to do with him – he couldn't play sports. The first film image Scorsese remembers seeing is Roy Rogers on Trigger. He found that he was able to communicate with his father through his father's love of the cinema. At some point, Scorsese became aware that there was somebody behind the camera making the films. For example, not every John Wayne film was great – they seemed to be much better when John Ford or Howard Hawks were the directors. The importance of film to Scorsese led him to seek a life in the cinema, and he often uses his encyclopaedic knowledge of films when directing. Rather than copy sequences outright, Scorsese tries to capture a feeling or mood that he remembered. During the filming of *The Age Of Innocence* he watched *Barry Lyndon* (Stanley Kubrick, 1975), *The Heiress* (William Wyler, 1949), *The Innocent* (Luchino Visconti, 1977) and many others, whilst for *Gangs Of New York* he watched Samuel Fuller, Sam Peckinpah and Sergio Leone. The opening battle sequence of *Gangs Of New York* echoes the gritty, gruelling fight from Orson Welles' little-seen masterpiece *Chimes At Midnight/Falstaff* (1966), whilst the closing duel is reminiscent of Akira Kurosawa's *Sanjuro* (1962). Scorsese lists 40 influential films in the book *Gangs Of New York: Making The Movie.*

Scorsese's love affair with film extends to the preservation and restoration of old films, as well as a willing participation in documentaries and publications that celebrate and explain film. (For a period of time he taught film at New York University.) The wealth of interview material with Scorsese is so overwhelming that it is both a joy and a frustration. A joy because Scorsese is very self-aware and likes to share. Frustrating because his view on the meaning and purpose of his films is often taken to be the defining view.

Analysis

*'There are men whom one hates until there comes a day when,
through a chink in their armour, you see something nailed down
and writhing in torment.'*

Gerald Kersh

The auteur theory proposed by François Truffaut and the
critics of *Cahiers Du Cinéma* says that the director is the
author of the work. This is often the case when directors
write all their own material, but how does it stand up for
somebody like Scorsese who has collaborated over many
years on differing projects with writers Mardik Martin,
Paul Schrader, Jay Cocks, Richard Price and Nicholas
Pileggi? (Not to mention cinematographers like Michael
Chapman, Michael Ballhaus and Robert Richardson,
editor Thelma Schoonmaker – veteran of 18 projects –
and many other collaborators.) As you can see from the
introduction to this book, the films often have consistent
themes. Similarly, there are recurring images and camera
movements. Here is an introduction to the various
sections used in this book.

Wiseguy: A recurring character in Scorsese's films is the
gangster, the confident criminal involved in organised
crime. These are based on people from Scorsese's old
neighbourhood, who hung around outside cafes in their
sharp suits and commanded respect. One of Scorsese's
early short films, *What's A Nice Girl Like You Doing In A
Place Like This?* (1963), features a wiseguy friend of the
central character who comments on the proceedings, and

his first feature film is also set in that world. Such is Scorsese's influence in this area that it is difficult to watch other films (like *Donnie Brasco* (dir Mike Newell, 1997)) and TV series (like *The Sopranos*) set in this milieu without thinking in terms of how Scorsese represented the characters.

Cine-Literate: The breadth and depth of Scorsese's film knowledge is astounding. He likes to watch a wealth of films whilst making films, and at the same time, like Truffaut, he often references movies and movie-making within the film.

Home Movie: Martin Scorsese didn't know what it was like to be an actor, so he decided to occasionally spend some time in front of the camera. This is why he turns up in his own movies, like *Boxcar Bertha* (1972), *Taxi Driver* and *After Hours*, and has even appeared in Akira Kurosawa's *Dreams* (1990) as Vincent Van Gogh. And Martin isn't the only Scorsese to appear. His mother, Catherine, appeared in the early shorts, and it became a sort of ritual for Scorsese to use her, his father Charlie and other friends and relatives in his films, both in front of and behind the camera.

Picture: There is a story that Catherine and Charlie Scorsese tell in Scorsese's affectionate family documentary *Italianamerican* (1974) about the portrait of one of their family. It is interesting to note that Scorsese often has a framed picture in his films, or a mural on the wall that he 'frames' with the camera, and that these often comment upon the film. The use of sand paintings over the titles of *Kundun*, for example, are symbols of the beauty, fragility and impermanence of the Tibetan society portrayed in the film.

Mirror Scenes: As a boy Scorsese used to act as his heroes in front of a mirror. Perhaps this is the root of the famous mirror scenes in *Taxi Driver* and *Raging Bull*.

Seeing: Scorsese has a very complex and malleable visual style that serves the story rather than stands apart from it. Good examples of this are the long tracking shots in *GoodFellas*. In the first we take Henry Hill's point of view as he walks around a bar talking to the characters he has grown up with. Henry's voice-over introduces us to the gangsters. The purpose of the shot is to show that Henry is completely integrated into this world. A later shot has Henry take girlfriend Karen into the Copacabana night-club via the kitchen. Many directors use this sort of long tracking shot for effect, but Scorsese has a purpose in mind. This is Henry showing off to Karen, and Karen being swept off her feet by the special treatment. We follow the couple into the club with the romantic pop song *Then He Kissed Me* by The Crystals playing. It is a feelgood shot and it ends with comedian Henny Youngman on stage telling jokes. As the one-liners keep coming on the soundtrack, Scorsese shows Henry and Tommy stealing almost half a million dollars. The two scenes flow into each other, continuing the feel-good atmosphere, and hence commenting upon the amoral excitement that the characters feel about their profession. This subtle, unobtrusive editing works like sleight of hand – allowing Scorsese to seamlessly bridge time and place with frightening ease. He and editor Thelma Schoonmaker are so good at this that they can command our complete attention with what is effectively a documentary on how to run a casino during the first 40 minutes of *Casino* (1995).

The visual vocabulary is so extensive that you can see why it takes Scorsese a year to edit his films. Even something as simple as an insert has meaning. When Henry is setting up the Air France robbery he meets the inside man in a bar. Henry looks over and gives the nod to Jimmy. The insert is a medium close-up of Jimmy seeing the nod and getting up. For this insert, Scorsese quickly moves the camera to Jimmy and speeds up the shot, giving a quick-zoom effect. It is obvious that Jimmy is nervous/excited by the nod. Scorsese is using the camera and editing to tell us that this is important if somebody as implacable as Jimmy is excited.

Another example is a sequence of three insert shots in *GoodFellas* after Henry gun-whips Karen's neighbour to a pulp after he assaulted Karen. This is Karen's introduction to the violent side of Henry's profession. Henry gives Karen the gun to hide. The first insert is of the bloody gun in her hand as she contemplates (in voice-over) what to do and decides that the excitement turns her on. The second insert is of the gun being put beside a bottle of milk in a milk tin. The third insert is of a wine glass being covered by a napkin just before Henry and Karen's feet come down to smash it – it is their wedding. So, in three short inserts Scorsese has shown us that Karen now accepts the gangster life and marries Henry. He follows the emotional progression of his characters rather than a plot-based one, which results in a non-linear film style that seems perfectly natural.

Hearing: The soundscapes of Scorsese's movies are just as complex as the picturescapes and they are completely integrated with the visuals. The overlapping of dialogue, ambient sounds and music between scenes makes his films feel like the last moments of a dying man as his life flashes before him. A voice-over often threads many scenes together, giving the films a distinctive point of view. This can be seen in *Taxi Driver*, but in *GoodFellas*, for example, Scorsese breaks the rule and has multiple voices. This creates a disorientating effect and completely fragments the narrative. (Scorsese's films are so rich in detail that a rigid narrative structure does not reveal itself until the end or with repeated viewings.)

Music is also very important to Scorsese. Besides his involvement as chief editor on the film of *Woodstock* (1970), he directed *The Last Waltz* (1978, The Band's last performance) and the Michael Jackson music video *Bad* (1987) as well as the musical *New York, New York* (1977). Right from the beginning, Scorsese selected popular songs so that they acted as point/counterpoint to sequences in his films. The right music adds atmosphere and, in the case of the films that play out over several decades, authenticity. Also the music can comment on the action and characters in an ironic fashion.

Subtext: Scorsese rarely directs films about love or

family. He concentrates on an individual, who is occasionally violent and who is angry with the corrupt society that is trapping him. His characters are workaholics, driven and feeling alienated from the people around them, including lovers, wives and family. We keep watching these people because we know that there is hope that these people will be redeemed and transformed by their experiences. That hope is rarely rewarded with a happy ending. Rather, we hope to gain a deeper emotional understanding of the characters.

For Scorsese, the redemption of his characters (or failure to be redeemed) alludes to the stories and iconography of the Roman Catholic Church. This is not surprising because Scorsese, who had been an altar boy and had grown up in awe of the mysteries of God, studied to be a priest but was thrown out because his grades were too low. He then enrolled at New York University with the intention of going back to become a priest, but he became so entranced with Haig Manoogian's film class that film became his new vocation in life.

As a child, Scorsese had been so inspired by the lavish Biblical epics that he had seen on the big screen, like *The Robe* (Henry Koster, 1953), *Samson And Delilah* (Cecil B DeMille, 1949) and *The Greatest Story Ever Told* (George Stevens, 1965), that he made up his own stories and drew them as comic strips, often in widescreen proportions. The title panels of his Biblical epic *The Eternal City* proclaim it is 'A Marso Production, presented in Marso Color.' Eventually, Scorsese and his close friends got hold of an 8mm camera and began making films of their own, like *Vesuvius VI* (1959), a mini epic of Ancient Rome.

Although it may not be obvious, religion plays a major role in Scorsese's development as a film artist, either as a celebration of its mystery (*The Last Temptation Of Christ* (1988), *Kundun*) or to retell the story of the prodigal son (*Taxi Driver, Raging Bull, GoodFellas*), or to explore aspects of its teachings in the modern world (*Who's That Knocking At My Door?, Mean Streets, Bringing Out The Dead*). *After Hours* could be seen as a reworking of Jesus' temptations in the desert transposed to New York – although I accept that's a bit of a stretch. In *Cape Fear* (1991), Max Cady is clad in religious tattoos whilst proclaiming that he is God's angel of retribution and vengeance. Scorsese used the crucifixion of Big Bill Shelly at the end of *Boxcar Bertha* shot-for-shot for the crucifixion of Jesus in *The Last Temptation Of Christ*.

Although his long career is full of great films executed in a variety of styles and genres, it is important to remember that Scorsese is tolerated by the Hollywood executives rather than embraced. Scorsese once quipped that instead of describing him as a Hollywood director he should be called an 'in spite of' Hollywood director. The fact is that he is a director who works on the edges of the main-stream, on personal projects, often forgoing his fee to offset production costs. He has been around for so long that he is often considered to be part of the mainstream, but his box office has been up and down. When it has been down, Scorsese is not so proud that he will not work for money. Although he has hit critical and financial high points with films like *Taxi Driver, Raging Bull* and *GoodFellas*, they are invariably followed by personal projects that fail to ignite the box office and Scorsese then works on superior Hollywood films like *The Color Of Money* or *Cape Fear* to regain his financial standing.

There was a period in the late 1980s and early 1990s when critics invariably referred to Martin Scorsese as America's greatest living director. Since that time directors as diverse as Michael Mann, David Lynch, Paul Thomas Anderson, Steven Spielberg and Steven Soderbergh have built a substantial body of work. It will be interesting to see if this will still be the case in twenty years' time.

1 Novice

"Films are my life."
Martin Scorsese

What's A Nice Girl Like You Doing In A Place Like This? (1963)

Cast: Zeph Michelis (Harry), Mimi Stark (Wife), Sarah Braveman (Analyst), Fred Sica (Friend), Robert Uricola (Singer), Frank Truglio (Photographer)

Crew: Director & Writer: Martin Scorsese, Cinematographer: Frank Truglio, Editor: Robert Hunsicker, Composer: Richard H Coll, B&W, 9 mins

Story: A writer, Algernon, who everybody calls Harry, buys a picture of a man fishing on a boat. He becomes obsessed by it and cannot stop looking at it, even when his friends are around. It prevents him from working, or is it a symbol for his writer's block? Harry falls for a girl who comes to his party. She's a painter, and she paints a beach with the sea coming in. Harry becomes obsessed with this picture and eventually falls into it.

Wiseguy: 'Friend' with dark glasses and a cigar.

Cine-Literate: Scorsese says that Mel Brooks' and Ernest Pintoff's animated short *The Critic* was the inspiration for this.

Home Movie: Catherine is in the party scene.

Picture: It's about two pictures!

Voice-Over: Harry.

Moral: "Life is fraught with peril."

Seeing: Scorsese always quotes the first two minutes of Francois Truffaut's *Jules Et Jim* (1961) as the place where you can learn a lot about storytelling. This short emulates that style, using still images, jump cutting, moving camera, animation and lighting effects to dazzling effect. So, from his very first film Scorsese does not tell a linear story but follows the thoughts and emotions of the central character to create a fragmented portrait.

Subtext: This is a story of meaningless obsession, of a person outside of society. Although Harry has many friends, and is intelligent, there is something inside him that makes him watch the pictures. Is Algernon/Harry a split personality, a Jekyll & Hyde in one person? It is also interesting to note that as well as the bright, fun loving crowd of friends, Harry has one wiseguy friend who is decidedly dark and dangerous. When Harry stares into the pictures, is Harry staring into a mirror? Or the unknowable? On another level, is this the story of Martin Scorsese, a man who obsesses about moving pictures, and concentrates on them to the detriment of those around him, eventually to fall into pictures and to become one himself? Or do the pictures represent a simple, tranquil escape from the frenetic pace and complications of the real world?

Background: Scorsese co-directed and edited *The Art Of Flamenco – Inesita* as part of his Film MA at New York University, before directing his first short.

Verdict: A surprisingly bright and surreal piece from Scorsese, which evokes some of the terror and paranoia of an Edgar Allan Poe short story. Or, more accurately, an Algernon Blackwood short story. 4/5

It's Not Just You, Murray! (1964)

Cast: Ira Rubin (Murray), San De Fazio (Joe), Andrea Martin (Wife), Robert Uricola (Singer), Catherine Scorsese (Mother), John Bicona, Victor Magnotta, Mardik Martin, Richard Sweeton, Bernard Weisberger

Crew: Director: Martin Scorsese, Writers: Mardik Martin, Martin Scorsese, Cinematographer: Richard H Coll, Editor: Eli F Bleich, Production Designers: Lancelot Braithwaite & Victor Magnotta, Composer: Richard H Coll, B&W, 15 mins

Story: Murray, a successful man, tells us his life story:

making gin during prohibition and laundering money. Basically, Murray does anything and everything his friend Joe tells him to do. For his trouble, he goes to jail, gets bones broken, that sort of thing. Murray is lucky to have met his lovely wife. Only Murray is so busy with business that he fails to notice that his best friend Joe ran out on him, is banging his wife behind his back, and is the father of Murray's children.

Wiseguy: Joe. Murray only thinks he's a wiseguy.

Cine-Literate: Slapstick scene à la François Truffaut's *Tirez Sur Le Pianiste*. Musical interlude. A man is shot just like Warner Brothers gangster movies of the 1930s (*The Roaring Twenties* (Raoul Walsh, 1939), *The Public Enemy* (William Wellman, 1931)). Ending is straight out of Federico Fellini's *8 1/2* (1963).

Home Movie: Catherine plays Murray's mother. Whenever Murray has a problem he wants to discuss with her she says, "Murray, eat first." She even feeds him spaghetti through the chicken wire in prison. The film was shot in Scorsese's grandmother's and uncle's apartments. Scorsese's older brother Frank appears in the final sequence.

Voice-Over: Murray.

Moral: "I always wanted to live good."

Seeing: Starts with a close-up of Murray. The comedy

arrest is one long hand-held shot. Many still photos. There is a mirror scene where Murray contemplates himself. It ends with a freeze frame of a flashbulb.

Subtext: Murray thinks that he is a big man and doesn't realise that he is a small cog in the mob machine. Joe is supposed to be Murray's friend, but he is using him. Murray does not think that he lives in a corrupt world. He does not realise that he is trapped. For him it is a gilded cage. The violence against himself and others is treated as a matter of business, and something comical. Murray is the nice guy and Joe is the villain. There is a point towards the end when Murray has an opportunity to confront Joe but Murray decides not to, whether it is out of friendship, or out of fear, or simply because Murray prefers to live in his fantasy world.

Background: Mardik Martin, an Armenian who grew up in Baghdad, arrived at NYU in 1959 and could not return to Iraq because the Iraqi revolution made it dangerous for him. He grew close to his only friend, Martin Scorsese, and helped him organise the 'plot' of *It's Not Just You, Murray!* The film won the Jesse L Lasky Intercollegiate Award and, most importantly, got Scorsese his degree. Scorsese was out of contact with main actor Ira Rubin for 25 years and then met him again on the set of *Life Lessons*, Scorsese's film for *New York Stories* (1989). As a result, Rubin got a speaking part.

Verdict: This is the first time that Scorsese used real stories from his neighbourhood in his films and it pays

dividends. Ira Rubin's hypnotic voice is ironically coun-
terpointed by images that clearly show Joe's machinations.
4/5

The Big Shave (1967)

Cast: Peter Bernuth (Young Man)

Crew: Director & Writer & Editor: Martin Scorsese,
Cinematographer: Ares Memertzis, Art Director: Ken
Gaulin, Special Effects: Eli F Bleich, 6 mins

Story: A man walks into an incredibly white bathroom
and starts shaving. He shaves again and again, drawing
blood. With his face and the wash basin covered in blood,
he looks at the mirror in approval.

Cine-Literate: The fetishistic way the reflections of the
porcelain and chrome bathroom are presented recall the
way Kenneth Anger shot the motorbike in *Scorpio Rising*
(1964).

Seeing: The film is one long mirror scene.

Hearing: 'I Can't Get Started With You' performed by
Bunny Berigan is a relaxing counterpoint to the violent
images.

Subtext: The nice, young man enters a clean world
(Vietnam), dirties it and hurts himself. When he looks at
himself in the mirror, he thinks the damage he has done

to himself is good. The man looks nice but is actually horrible. His behaviour is obsessive and violent. 'Viet '67' appears in the credits, and Scorsese has said in interviews that this film is a metaphor for the war. He also credits the whiteness to Herman Melville, referring to the white whale, Moby Dick, which is a metaphor for obsession.

The idea for *The Big Shave* came to Scorsese during a period of depression when he had trouble shaving. He wanted to make the film as a protest against the Vietnam war, but it was also about his personal demons. The young man is obsessed and ignores everything around him, believing himself to be untouched by the world, in the same manner as Harry and Murray in Scorsese's previous short films. Was Scorsese beginning to think that this man was him?

Background: Scorsese married fellow student Laraine Marie Brennan and they had a daughter on 7 December 1965. He began teaching at NYU and encouraged his students in the same way as his mentor Haig Manoogian. Scorsese got a grant for *The Big Shave* from Jacques Ledoux, curator of the Cinémathèque Royale de Belgique in Brussels, and the film won the Prix L'Age d'Or at Ledoux's Festival of Experimental Cinema in Knokke-le-Zoute in December 1967.

Verdict: A hermetic surreal masterpiece. A simple idea superbly executed. 5/5

Who's That Knocking At My Door? (1968)

Cast: Harvey Keitel (JR), Zina Bethune (The Young Girl), Lennard Kuras (Joey), Michael Scala (Sally GaGa), Bill Minkin (Iggy), Harry Northup (Rapist), Anne Collette (Young Girl in Dream), Catherine Scorsese (JR's Mother), Robert Uricola (Gunman)

Crew: Director & Writer: Martin Scorsese, Cinematographers: Richard H Coll, Michael Wadleigh, Max Fisher, Editor: Thelma Schoonmaker, B&W, 90 mins

Alternative Titles: *Bring On The Dancing Girls* (1965), *I Call First* (1967), *JR* (1970)

Story: JR and Joey get involved with a fight, then go to Joey's bar. Joey slaps around his barman Sally GaGa, who is always taking money. As Joey talks and makes plans to go uptown to see a prostitute, JR thinks about the girl he met waiting for the Staten Island ferry. He chats her up by talking about the movies. In his bedroom, they kiss for a long time but he stops them going further. "I love you," he tells her, and explains that he's old fashioned. Later, he explains that there are two kinds of women, girls (i.e. virgins, who you marry) and broads (i.e. whores, who you don't marry). The Girl tells JR that a former boyfriend raped her, and JR asks her, "How can I believe this story?" and she leaves. After a drunken party with some friends and a broad, JR visits the Girl at her apartment to say, "I understand now and I forgive you. I'll marry you anyway." The Girl finds this attitude unacceptable so she rejects him. JR goes to church to get rid of his sins. When he kisses the feet of Jesus, the feet bleed – Jesus suffers for JR's sins.

Wiseguy: Gangster at the party puts gun to Sally GaGa's head.

Cine-Literate: JR chats up the girl by talking about John Wayne, Jeffrey Hunter and Natalie Wood in *The Searchers* (John Ford, 1956). He takes the girl to see *Rio Bravo* (Howard Hawks, 1959), and explains why Lee Marvin is a villain in *The Man Who Shot Liberty Valance* (John Ford, 1962): "He was the worst kind of bad guy. Not only does he kill people but he breaks furniture."

Home Movie: Martin Scorsese plays a gangster at the party. Catherine Scorsese is JR's mother and does some cooking.

Voice-Over: JR.

Moral: "It was great at the top but boy getting to the top is murder."

Picture: Nude girl over the bar. Dignified looking man in picture in JR's mother's kitchen.

Seeing: When JR first talks with the Girl, it is one long take. There are many slow pans across the bar, and the parties. The most effective is the gangster party, when successive slow motion pans from left to right are closer and closer to the gangsters. When the gun goes off, we cut to still images from the Western *Rio Bravo*. Later, when showing the rape, Scorsese uses still images. JR and the Girl come out of the cinema and walk down the street in a reverse tracking shot with the cinema in the background. There are several God shots, looking down on the world – sometimes JR and the Girl are on the roof looking down on the people below, emphasising their separation from JR's world. The film is full of religious imagery and paraphernalia: crucifixes, statues of saints, and the holy candle. Significantly, at one point the Girl blows out a holy candle, which represents the religious doctrine that she is trying to snuff out in JR.

The 'dream sequence' where JR sleeps with many whores is like a mini film. It begins with a close-up of JR's face in many jumpcuts. Then JR reclines naked on a bed (like a reclining crucifixion) with a half-dressed woman walking up and down the room. There is much sex, with the camera circling the entwined couple (à la Hitchcock's *Vertigo*), before the sequence ends with the positions reversed: the woman is naked on the bed and JR is dressed. JR then flicks a pack of cards at the woman.

Hearing: The music is integral to this film because it is an ironic counterpoint to the actions. However, in the rape scene, the music becomes distorted which adds to the discord. In contrast, when JR and the Girl kiss for a long time in his bedroom, the intimate images are accompanied by natural ambient sound which gives it a sweet intensity.

Subtext: Within this devoutly Roman Catholic Italian-American society, women are considered to be either virgins or whores, girls or broads. JR is trapped by this concept and cannot fight it. He lives in two worlds – the world of lightness with the Girl, or the world of darkness, alcohol, violence and sexual depravity with his male friends. Consequently, JR becomes a Jekyll & Hyde character. This is shown explicitly when he stands in front of his bedroom mirror before kissing the Girl – as he walks away from the mirror, the other half of him in the mirror is separated from him. JR's fight to achieve serenity is shown in metaphor by his day trip to the country with Joey. They spend three hours in a bar in Copake because Joey wants to drink, then their guide (who represents JR's good nature) leads them to the top of a mountain. Joey complains constantly, trying to make JR stop so that they go back down. Eventually, all three get to the top. Joey cannot understand what all the fuss is about. JR marvels at the view and he says in voice-over, "It was great at the top but boy getting to the top is murder."

The film is about juxtaposing opposites in images and actions. The first shot of the movie has JR's mother baking in her kitchen. This is a nice image but it is accompanied by a metallic thumping sound that makes it violent. The next scene is upbeat dance music with images of boys beating the shit out of each other. The next set of scenes contrast Joey, JR and Sally GaGa going to see a prostitute with JR flirting with the Girl waiting for the Staten Island ferry. Then we have Sally GaGa kissing a girl whilst stealing the money from her purse, followed by JR kissing the Girl and stopping them from going all the way. Next is a violent party with gangsters shot in beautiful slow motion and soothing music, which contrasts with JR's

violent, quickly-edited sex scenes to the rhythm of The
Doors performing 'The End.' The first line of 'The End' is
'The killer awoke before dawn.' (This predates Francis
Ford Coppola's famous use of the song in *Apocalypse Now*
by 10 years.) JR's hypocritical attitude to sex is highlighted
– when the Girl tells him about the time she was raped, it
is portrayed as a violent act, yet JR does not believe her
and says she knew what she was getting into. Then there is
a party scene where JR and his friends joke and play
around as they take turns with two broads. The last two
scenes play with the idea of forgiveness. JR knocks on the
Girl's high-class apartment in the clouds, and she lets him
in. JR says that he forgives her for her sin and that he'll
marry her anyway. When she rejects him, he calls her a
broad and a whore. This contrasts with the following scene
in a church where, while the soundtrack pumps out
'Who's That Knocking At My Door?', JR asks for forgiveness and hopes to avoid sin in the future. The point is that
JR would never fully forgive the Girl for her sin, yet he
believes that he would be forgiven for all the hurt he
causes others.

Background: After *It's Not Just You, Murray!* Scorsese
decided to take his Masters at NYU and it was at this stage
that an autobiographical trilogy germinated in his mind.
The first part, *Jerusalem, Jerusalem*, told of JR going on a
religious retreat where he reimagines the stories of Jesus as
modern-day stories of a New York criminal. The film was
never made because Scorsese decided to make the second
part of the trilogy, which was eventually called *Who's That
Knocking At My Door?* Since there was no real money, the

cast and crew worked during the week to earn money for rent and food and then filmed over the weekends. The first version ran 58 minutes and didn't work because it didn't have a story, although all the material about the boys hanging out together was natural. Haig Manoogian put money towards a second version that was filmed three years later. Harvey Keitel was the only actor to return from the first version and he was joined by Zina Bethune as The Girl, Mike Wadleigh as cameraman and Thelma Schoonmaker as editor. This version won Best Student Film at the Chicago Film Festival but couldn't get a distribution deal. Eventually, a distributor said he'd take it if they added a nude scene. Keitel flew over to Amsterdam whilst Scorsese was in Europe and they filmed the very effective dream sequence. The film got distribution.

Verdict: This is a good film to see if you want to spot images and ideas that reoccur in later Scorsese films. It has startling individual scenes but fails to gel as a whole. Having said that, the film has an authenticity that is appealing and is not unlike the work of John Cassavetes. 2/5

Street Scenes (1970)

Cast: Many people including Harvey Keitel (Himself), Martin Scorsese (Interviewer)

Crew: Director: Martin Scorsese, Cinematographers: Bill Etra, Tiger Graham, Fred Hadley, Don Lenzer, Bob Pitts, Peter Rea, Danny Schneider, Edward Summer, Nat Tripp,

Editors: Angela Kirby, Maggie Koven, Gerry Pallor, Peter Rea, Thelma Schoonmaker, Larry Tisdall, Sound: Harry Peck Bolles

Background: In 1968, Scorsese was given a $150,000 budget to make a black and white film called *The Honeymoon Killers*, based on a true story. He started shooting his 200-page script in master shots, i.e. one long shot without any inserts or coverage. This meant that he didn't have any close-ups or footage to insert to vary the angle or rhythm of the scenes. He was fired after a week. The producer Leonard Kastle took over the direction and made a pretty good job of it.

Moving from job to job (e.g. supplying tough American dialogue for Dutch film *Bezeten – Het gat in de muur* (aka *Obsessions*, Pim de la Parra, 1969), Scorsese became an Assistant Instructor at NYU. One August weekend in 1969, Scorsese went to Woodstock to assist Michael Wadleigh film a continuous three-day music festival that became legendary. Scorsese was an assistant director and also worked on the editing under Thelma Schoonmaker. They had no food and no toilets. The cameras kept breaking down because of the humidity. Nobody had any idea who was playing and when. It was kept afloat by the spirit of the event. And to think, the always dapper Scorsese had brought along cufflinks because, you know, he thought it'd be that kind of event.

The late 1960s saw lots of student demonstrations for civil rights and protests against war, some of which resulted in confrontations with the police. Scorsese and his students formed the New York Cinetracts Collective and demanded to be given equipment by NYU to document the upheavals. *Street Scenes* was footage they took at an anti-war demonstration in Washington, a march on Wall Street, discussions, confrontations and polemics.

Fred Weintraub of Warner Brothers had bought *Woodstock* (1970) and had over 9 hours of footage that needed editing down for *Medicine Ball Caravan* (1971), François Reichenbach's record of a 154-strong troupe of musicians who had toured America to spread peace and love. This two-week job turned into 9 months, so this is how Scorsese arrived in Hollywood. This is where Scorsese cemented his relationships with Brian De Palma and John Cassavetes, and forged new ones with Francis Ford Coppola, George Lucas and Steven Spielberg. When work dried up, Cassavetes hired Scorsese as sound editor on *Minnie And Moskcowitz* (1971). Once Scorsese held Cassavetes steady as somebody hit him to record sound effects for a fight. Scorsese had trouble adjusting to LA and living on his own, so he slept on the set because it was less depressing.

Boxcar Bertha (1972)

Cast: Barbara Hershey ('Boxcar' Bertha Thompson), David Carradine ('Big' Bill Shelly), Barry Primus (Rake Brown), Bernie Casey (Von Morton), John Carradine (H Buckram Sartoris), Victor Argo (McIver #1), David R Osterhout (McIver #2), Grahame Pratt (Emeric Pressburger), 'Chicken' Holleman (M Powell), Harry Northup (Harvey Hall), Ann Morell (Tillie Parr), Marianne Dole (Mrs Mailler), Joe Reynolds (Joe Cox)

Crew: Director: Martin Scorsese, Writers: Joyce H
Corrington & John William Corrington, Book: *Sisters Of
The Road* by Bertha Thompson & Ben L Reitman,
Producers: Samuel Z Arkoff (Executive), James H
Nicholson (Executive), Julie Corman (Associate), Roger
Corman, Cinematographer: John Stephens, Editor: Buzz
Feitshans, Composers: Gib Guilbeau, Thad Maxwell, 92
mins

Story: Depression era America. Bertha's father is killed in
an aeroplane accident whilst trying to earn money crop-
spraying. In the ensuing chaos Von (the black plane engineer) and Bill Shelly (a railroad worker putting down rails
nearby) fight with the landowner to protect Bertha.
Afterwards, she lives in the hobo camps and travels on the
empty boxcars of the Reader railroad. She meets Bill
again, falls in love with him and is eventually sucked into
a life of crime with Bill (after leading the union against the
railroad, the railroad are trying to kill him), Von and
gambler Rake Brown.

After stealing a payroll from a train, Bill's conscience
can't handle being a criminal, so he gives his share of the
money to the union. The union accept the money but say
that Bill is no longer wanted. The next time the gang hold
up the railway payroll they make sure the employees get
$10 extra in each pay packet. After hijacking a big party
given by railroad chief, H Buckram Sartoris, Sartoris sets a
trap. Rake is killed, Bertha escapes, and Bill and Von are
jailed.

To survive, Bertha becomes a prostitute. A long time
passes, and then she hears Von's familiar harmonica. Von

takes her to Bill at their hideout. As they meet, the railroad men attack. Bertha is beaten. Bill is crucified to a boxcar. Von attacks and kills the railroad men but is too late to save Bill. The train departs, and Bertha runs after Bill.

Wiseguy: Rake Brown perhaps? He's a small time gambler from the big city.

Cine-Literate: When Bertha is at a cinema foyer, the main film poster behind her is *The Man Who Could Work Miracles* (Lothar Mendes, 1936) – perhaps her interpretation of her ideal man, Bill, who is the messiah figure of the movie. Two of the characters are called Powell and Pressburger, after one of Scorsese's favourite film-making teams.

Home Movie: Scorsese plays a brothel client who asks Bertha if he could stay the night if he pays her a few dollars extra.

Picture: There is a trick picture in H Buckram Sartoris' office. When seen from different angles different presidents are shown.

Seeing: One of the opening shots is a close-up of Bertha, with her father's aeroplane superimposed over her face. Not only do we get to see what she is looking at, but we get the metaphor for the story – this is about freedom. When the camera pans across the jail, picking out each man, we get a precursor to Scorsese's trademark 'introduction' shot. This pan is repeated at the party. When Bill decides to give the money to the union, there is a dramatic reverse tracking shot from low-down on the floor. The hand-held camera roams through the ruins of a house as we hear the lovemaking of Bertha and Bill. When Rake's playing cards fall on the floor, Bertha picks up the ace of hearts and puts it in Bill's breast pocket. This card is nailed above Bill in the final crucifixion scene. The image of Bill crucified to a boxcar and being carried away from Bertha is symbolic of the way the railroad has taken away Bertha's partner from her. This religious imagery is echoed earlier; when Bill is 'preaching' to his gang about morality there is a painting of Jesus behind him.

Hearing: The film opens with Von (a black man and skilled aeroplane engineer) playing a harmonica with Bill and his co-workers (white labourers) hitting the rail spikes to the same rhythm. This immediately creates a bond between them. Later, Bill recognises Von in jail when he hears his soulful harmonica. Told to play 'Dixie' by the Sheriff, Von plays it in a blues style, completely subverting the Sheriff's intention. Later, when Bertha is walking the streets, she hears Von's harmonica playing and walks into a black-only bar. The reactions of the blacks show that she is not welcome, but she is unaware of this because she associates the music with her friend. The blues music binds the oppressed (whether black or white) together.

Subtext: Corrupt Society – The film portrays all forms of law (police) and business (landowner, railroad) as corrupt. Also, as Bill discovers, the union is corrupt because it is willing to take his stolen money. In the end, they can only rely on each other. Trapped By Society – All the characters are looking for freedom. Bill wants better wages and conditions but becomes a common thief. He is already an outlaw from society, but he must decide whether or not to remain true to his principles. When he decides to kidnap H Buckram Sartoris, he is caught and crucified, thus becoming a martyr. Bertha's desires are unclear since she never expresses them. She has sex with many men, and uses sex to distract a guard, but she only loves Bill. Von knows and accepts his lowly position within society, so he remains constant throughout the film. He comes to the defence of Bertha on two occasions – the death of her father and the death of her lover. Violence – The film begins with a fistfight to defend Bertha, and then the fights are to do with the strike (Bill inciting violence), race (the jail riot starts because the Sheriff does not like Bill shaking hands with Von) and revenge (the final shootout because Bill has been crucified). Jekyll & Hyde – Bill is ruled by his mind and acts out of principle. Bertha acts because of her emotions so when she kills, it is impulsive. She is also playful with violence. During one hold-up she repeatedly makes the McIvers stand up and sit down at gunpoint.

Background: Scorsese was working as a sound editor on John Cassavete's *Minnie And Moskowitz* when Roger Corman, who had seen and liked *Who's That Knocking At My Door?*, offered him a sequel to *Bloody Mama* (Roger Corman, 1970) called *Boxcar Bertha*. Scorsese was given a budget of $600,000, 24 days to shoot on location in Arkansas and a script that bore little relation to Bertha

Thompson's autobiography. Corman told Scorsese that he could rewrite but there must be some kind of nudity or sexual frisson every 15 minutes. Scorsese felt insecure dealing with such an alien subject so Rake Brown was rewritten as a New York gambler to become a sort of Scorsese alter ego. Also, afraid that he would be fired, Scorsese prepared the shoot by drawing every shot of the movie – about 500 pictures. Although he might not use them, they were there for him to fall back on. Whilst filming on location, Roger Corman arrived to make sure everything was going well. He told Scorsese not to worry, that he was going to walk around and scowl at everybody to get them back on their toes. Corman pointed out that *Bonnie And Clyde* (Arthur Penn, 1967) had a car chase but there was no car chase in the picture, so Scorsese had to add it, on location, without any extra money or time. The car chase was a staple of the Depression era gangster exploitation flick created by *Bonnie And Clyde* and perpetuated by films like *Thieves Like Us* (Robert Altman, 1973), *The Grissom Gang* (Robert Aldritch, 1971) and *Bloody Mama*.

At the end of the shoot, Barbara Hershey and David Carradine gave Scorsese a book by Nikos Kazantzakis called *The Last Temptation Of Christ*. He liked it so much, it took him seven years to finish reading it.

Verdict: Although this goes some way to evoke the atmosphere of the Depression, and tries to use the background of union strikes to justify the actions of the main characters, it fails because there is no focus. We follow Bertha around, but we learn very little about her. As a result, the film lacks a moral focus, which is how Scorsese usually tells his stories. All the characters are ill-defined, perhaps because the storyline jumps from place to place in order to get as much sex and violence into the film as possible. The whole thing is fascinating to watch as an early Scorsese film but it is a bit clunky. 2/5

Back in New York, Scorsese showed a two-hour rough cut to John Cassavettes, who took Scorsese aside, said that he had spent a year of his life making a piece of shit, that he'd loved *Who's That Knocking At My Door?* and that Scorsese should work on something that he believed in. Scorsese got out his script for the sequel *Season Of The Witch* and decided to rewrite it.

2 Doing The Right Thing

"You don't make up for your sins in church. You do it in the streets. You do it at home. The rest is bullshit and you know it."

> Charlie (spoken by Martin Scorsese)
> talking to God, *Mean Streets* (1973)

Mean Streets (1973)

Cast: Harvey Keitel (Charlie), Robert De Niro (Johnny Boy Cervello), David Proval (Tony), Amy Robinson (Teresa), Richard Romanus (Michael), Cesare Danova (Giovanni), Victor Argo (Mario), George Memmoli (Joey Clams), Lenny Scaletta (Jimmy), Jeannie Bell (Diane), Murray Moston (Oscar), David Carradine (Drunk), Robert Carradine (Boy with Gun), Harry Northup (Jerry the Soldier)

Crew: Director & Story: Martin Scorsese, Writers: Martin Scorsese & Mardik Martin, Producers: E Lee Perry (Executive), Jonathan T Taplin, Cinematographer: Kent Wakeford, Editor: Sid Levin, Composers: Eric Clapton, Bert Holland, Mick Jagger, Keith Richards, 110 mins

Story: In a series of character-led incidents set against the background of New York's Italian community, book ended by the start and conclusion of the San Gennaro Festival, we follow the life of Charlie, a small-time member of the wiseguy community who collects protection money. His friends Tony and Michael are part of the community, but his other friend Johnny Boy is unreliable and therefore must be shunned. Charlie's secret girlfriend has epilepsy, and so must also be shunned. When Charlie's uncle Giovanni offers him a restaurant – the first step up the ladder – Charlie is forced to choose between his desire for power, his love for Teresa and his duty to protect his friend Johnny Boy.

Wiseguy: This is a movie full of wiseguys. Tony is the fiery but fair bar owner. Michael is the businessman who will not allow anything to stand in the way of his acquiring money. Charlie, the central character, is the politician who wants to gain respect. Uncle Giovanni is the godfather of the community.

Cine-Literate: When Michael and Tony con $20 from two kids from Riverdale, they go to the movies with Charlie to see *The Searchers* (John Ford, 1956) and watch a knockabout fight scene. This echoes the many fights the wiseguys have with each other. Charlie tells Teresa that one of his favourite things is John Wayne, which links the film with *Who's That Knocking At My Door?* Later Charlie goes to see *The Tomb Of Ligeia* (Roger Corman, 1964) with Johnny Boy. We see the fiery climax of the doomed Vincent Price, which resonates with the feeling of doom that is beginning to surround Charlie. Also, Scorsese worked for Corman. In the final sequence, the car crashes and we see a clip from *The Big Heat* (Fritz Lang, 1953) where Glenn Ford holds the dead body of his wife after his car explodes. The implication is that Teresa will die in the crash.

Home Movie: Martin as Jimmy Shorts appears three times in the background before shooting Johnny Boy at the end. In a nice touch, Scorsese kisses the gun before he fires. Catherine is the woman who helps Teresa when she has an epileptic fit.

Picture: There is a painting of a naked woman in Tony's bar, as in *Who's That Knocking At My Door?* Most of the pictures we see on the walls of the shops and homes are religious.

Voice-Over: Scorsese's voice substitutes Charlie's thoughts.

Seeing: The film begins where *Who's That Knocking At My Door?* ends, in Old St Patrick's Church where Scorsese was once an altar boy. At the beginning, when the music cuts in, Scorsese cuts to the beat, cutting to a closer shot with each beat – it is a speeded-up version of one of Akira Kurosawa's trademark edits, and also echoes the editing style of the dream sequence in *Who's That Knocking At My Door* In a shot that has now become a trademark, Scorsese moves the camera through a red-lit bar in slow motion. (The colour red was predominant in the films of Powell and Pressburger.) During the pool-room fight, there are long takes following the people around the room as they beat each other up. When the group welcome a friend back from Vietnam, they all get drunk – Scorsese strapped a camera to Keitel as he moves around getting progressively drunk. It is a great effect.

Hearing: There is a constant bombardment of rock and pop music both as a soundtrack and as background noise. Scorsese takes care to layer the sound environment of the characters so that we also hear the music from the San Gennaro Festival. The film plays out with the ironic (bitter?) 'There's No Place Like Home.'

Subtext: As Scorsese/Charlie explains in the church, there are two kinds of pain in Hell – the pain you feel with your hand and the pain you feel in your heart. Throughout the movie Charlie, or 'Saint Charles' as he is once called, holds his hand over a flame (a candle, an oven fire, a lit tumbler of whiskey) to feel the pain of Hell, and indeed at the climax he is shot in the hand, but the spiritual pain of his conscience hurts him more. (Tony also hurts his right hand during the film.) He has failed to commit to a relationship to Teresa, and he has failed to protect his friend Johnny Boy, because of the rules of the society he belongs to.

Charlie was told by Giovanni to distance himself from Teresa and Johnny Boy if he wants to progress because "honourable men go with honourable men." Charlie's disobedience is a 'sin' against this society and the shootout at the end can be seen as the wrath of that society being visited upon Charlie. This is prefigured by the story told to Charlie and Tony by the priests at a retreat – a novice priest and nun have sex in a car before taking their final vows but during the act they are killed. Charlie believes the story and consequently believes in the wrath of God.

Mean Streets then is about Charlie's fear of God (Charlie: "You don't fuck around with the infinite") and his fear of the wiseguy society. These two fears tear him apart because he wants to appease both sides, like his hero St Francis of Assisi. As Johnny Boy says, "Everybody loves Charlie. He's a fucking politician." Or, more pointedly, Johnny Boy calls him "two-faced." Scorsese alludes to this Jekyll & Hyde existence by constantly having Charlie stand in front of mirrors to examine himself and ponder his next move.

Although this is a corrupt society, the people within it obviously do not think it is. Only Teresa seems to point this out to Charlie, who feels increasingly trapped by the wiseguy community. He does not feel threatened because all the characters are friends. The violence is very 'John Ford,' i.e. accepted and treated casually. People rarely get seriously hurt (except when a drunk is shot – David Carradine in a cameo role). Then the violence escalates at the climax. Like the shooting of the drunk, it is a matter of business and respect for men of honour.

In the end it must be acknowledged that Charlie is fooling himself into thinking that he can remain moral in an immoral world, but he is actually a snob (he will not do manual work but he expects Johnny Boy to do it), he is repressed (he does not express himself freely as Johnny

Boy does) and a misogynist (he will not acknowledge that Teresa is his girlfriend and hints that he will not marry her because she is not a virgin – as in *Who's That Knocking At My Door?*). He is reminiscent of Harry Fabian in Jules Dassin's *Night And The City* (1950), a morally reprehensible villain and coward, who wants to get rich quick without earning it, but who seeks to redeem himself in the end.

Background: After about 27 rewrites, Scorsese eventually got *Season Of The Witch* into shape. His friend Jay Cocks renamed it *Mean Streets* after the famous Raymond Chandler quote. After rejecting Roger Corman's offer to distribute a black cast version to cash in on the emerging blaxploitation genre, Scorsese got financing through Jonathan Taplin, former road manager for Bob Dylan and The Band. Jon Voight (still in demand after *Midnight Cowboy* (John Schlesinger, 1969)) turned down the lead so Scorsese recast Harvey Keitel as the Scorsese alter ego. Robert De Niro, who had appeared in various Brian De Palma films and who had grown up a couple of streets away from Scorsese, was persuaded to take the part of Johnny Boy. There were weeks of rehearsal in New York, where some of the great dialogue scenes were improvised between the cast and then transcribed. Six days and nights of location work followed in New York (to film hallways and street shots – the San Gennaro Festival was filmed the previous October with Harvey Keitel) including Catherine Scorsese's kitchen. The interiors were filmed in Los Angeles to save on costs. The final shootout was based on an incident when Scorsese and Joey Gaga (the basis for

Johnny Boy) were riding in a red convertible. After they were dropped off, they heard shots and ran after the car. The driver had got into an argument and one of the passengers was shot in the eyes, and lived. The resulting award-winning film effectively launched the careers of Scorsese, Keitel and De Niro. *Mean Streets* was remade after a fashion by Hong Kong auteur Wong Kar-Wai as *Wong Gok Ka Moon* (*As Tears Go By*, 1988).

Verdict: In the early 1970s, directors like Sidney Lumet (*Serpico* 1973) and William Friedkin (*The French Connection* 1971) brought a gritty realism to the New York milieu, but it was the emotional and psychological grittiness of John Cassavetes' films that comes through in *Mean Streets*. This is a complex street fable where the ritual of Michael complaining about Johnny Boy, Charlie smoothing things over and everybody having a friendly drink is repeated until it explodes. 4/5

Italianamerican (1974)

Cast: Catherine Scorsese, Charles Scorsese, Martin Scorsese

Crew: Director: Martin Scorsese, Writers: Larry Cohen, Mardik Martin, Producers: Elaine Attias, Saul Rubin, Bert Lovitt (Associate), Cinematographer: Alec Hirschfeld, Editor: Bert Lovitt, 45 mins

Home Movie: Martin Scorsese interviews his mum and dad about their life in New York and the family history back in Sicily. As they talk, mum makes meatballs and we get the recipe as part of the end credits.

Picture: A portrait of a relative in uniform forms the basis of a story.

Seeing: Lots of handheld camerawork mixed with historical footage and family photos.

Subtext: These are two people who have lived together for a long time and know each other very well. They have retained individual identities and differing opinions, yet have found a way to live with each other.

Background: Scorsese directed this for a TV series about American immigrants called *Storm Of Strangers*. It was a personal turning point because the distance of the camera allowed him to see his parents as people involved in a love story rather than as parents. Also, the documentary form forced Scorsese to 'make' a story out of pieces of film without having to follow a story form. This freedom is something that Scorsese uses in many of his subsequent films. By combining voice-overs and images, Scorsese can jump time and place in an instant, bringing him closer to a mental form, i.e. following thoughts and emotions rather than following a story.

Verdict: Both Catherine and Charles are fascinating storytellers. Their idiosyncrasies are endearing. 3/5

Alice Doesn't Live Here Anymore (1974)

Cast: Mia Bendixsen (Alice, Age 8), Ellen Burstyn (Alice Hyatt), Alfred Lutter (Tommy Hyatt), Billy Green Bush (Donald), Lelia Goldoni (Bea), Ola Moore (Old Woman), Harry Northup (Joe & Jim's Bartender), Harvey Keitel (Ben), Diane Ladd (Flo), Vic Tayback (Mel), Valerie Curtin (Vera), Kris Kristofferson (David), Jodie Foster (Audrey/Doris), Laura Dern (Girl Eating Ice Cream Cone)

Crew: Director: Martin Scorsese, Writer: Robert Getchell, Producers: Audrey Maas, David Susskind, Sandra Weintraub (Associate), Cinematographer: Kent L Wakeford, Editor: Marcia Lucas, Composer: Richard LaSalle, 112 mins

Story: When Alice Hyatt is widowed after years of domesticity, she decides to travel to Monterey with her 11-year-old son Tommy to resume a singing career. In Phoenix, Arizona she sings at a piano bar and starts a relationship with Ben, who turns out to be violent. In Tucson, she gives up her dream of singing and becomes a waitress. She falls for a farmer, David, and repeats her fall into domesticity.

Cine-Literate: The opening sequence is stylised to look like the Kansas farm in *The Wizard Of Oz* (Victor Fleming, 1939), and the young Alice looks like Dorothy. The story of Dorothy following the yellow brick road echoes Alice's road trip to follow her dreams. When Ben tries to cuddle up close to Alice she resists, then Scorsese cuts to Betty Grable in *Coney Island* (Walter Lang, 1943), singing 'Cuddle Up A Little Closer, Lovey Mine' – the film is a rags-to-riches story of a saloon entertainer becoming a musical star, which reflects Alice's ambition. The film has a sexual connotation when Alice talks to Bea about the size of Robert Redford's manhood, and to David about kissing in *The Postman Always Rings Twice* (Tay Garnett, 1946). Tommy, dressed as a cowboy, emulates Yul Brynner in *Westworld* (Michael Crichton, 1973) or perhaps John Wayne.

Picture: When Alice sits down to dinner with trucker husband Donald, there is a picture of a road on the wall – a hint of the journey to come. At the motel in Tucson, there is a picture of the sea on the wall – Alice intends to go to Monterey, which is on the coast. David's idealistic credentials are evident by the picture of John F Kennedy and Robert F Kennedy on the wall of his house.

Seeing: The film opens with a stylised film of Alice's past being projected onto the black screen, just as *Mean Streets* began with home movies projected onto a black screen. There are several long crane shots, the first high over Socorro, then over a street, then into Alice's house. Another over a bridge lowers to reveal Donald's crashed truck. There is a reverse tracking shot of Alice looking for work in Phoenix. When she begins work at Mel and Ruby's diner in Tucson there is a good shot of Flo quickly serving plates of food to the customers. Later, when Alice breaks up with David, a long hand-held shot in the diner leads her out of the dining room, through the kitchen, into the back and then into the ladies' toilets. The simplicity and directness of all these shots make them almost invisible and not at all showy. Scorsese likes to do inserts of hand gestures. We have inserts of Alice's friends' hands clasping hers in condolence, and of Alice doing a 'chop-chop' gesture to tell Tommy to scram. Ben points his hand at Alice like a gun, which is a prelude of the violence to come (his job is to pack powder into bullets). There are similar shots in *Mean Streets* (Giovanni) and *Taxi Driver* (the salesman swiping his hand over the guns). There are many mirror scenes, partly to overcome the logistical problem of filming in small motels. Perhaps the shot of Alice shaving her legs is a homage to *The Big Shave*? Or perhaps not.

Hearing: Alice's melodic ballads are in direct contrast to Tommy's rhythmic Mott The Hoople and T-Rex. Although mother and son fool around a lot, they are often out of sync with each other.

Subtext: Alice is trapped by her conflicting and contrary desires. On the one hand she wants to sing because she was happy singing (even though she knows she is not that great), but she is attracted to "strong and dominating" men, the kind of selfish men who do not understand her desires. Her husband Donald does not communicate with her (Alice makes a joke of this by holding a conversation and doing both their voices), and is short-tempered with their annoying brat of a child Tommy, but when she cries in bed you can see that Donald also has tears in his eyes.

Young, amusing Ben is also strong and dominating but in a violent way. Once Alice recognises this, she makes a run for it. This is why she is so wary when David asks her out. David has an artistic side (he plays guitar), is idealistic (the JFK/RFK picture), is knowledgeable and sensitive, yet he is also forceful. When his wife left him with their children, he held the door open for them. He can be abrupt (he asks Alice to serve him before she gives him news) and practical (he will not ruin his truck just so that Tommy can go fishing), but he also smacks Tommy when he is naughty. This last incident causes a break-up between Alice and David because Alice spoils Tommy. She wants to be his friend rather than his mother, and tolerates and plays with him as a fellow child. Perhaps what she truly desires is a father figure. David represents a middle ground between Donald and Ben.

Alice's hypocrisy/repression is shown in her attitude to swearing. As a child she swears, as Tommy swears. As an adult she also swears a lot, yet admonishes Tommy for swearing. At the diner, she considers Flo to be vulgar because of her swearing. When Alice eventually laughs at one of Flo's vulgar expressions it is a sign that Alice has at last begun to rid herself of her repressions.

As for Monterey, it is a symbol of the last time Alice was truly happy. David asks her whether she wants to go there because she wants to go home, or because she wants to sing. When David offers to sell his farm so that she can live there and perhaps sing, Alice realises that she has found the right man. He may not completely understand her, but at least he is willing to go some way to make her happy. She does not need to be in Monterey, only to feel as she did when she was there. The film ends with Alice and Tommy preparing to make a life with David in Tucson, the sign for the Monterey Dining Room ahead of them in the distance implying the happy future they had been seeking.

Background: Flush with the critical (if not financial) success of *Mean Streets*, Scorsese was offered his first studio picture, a melodrama. Ellen Burstyn (hot from the financial success of *The Exorcist* (William Friedkin, 1973)) picked the project and picked Scorsese for the job because she wanted a new, edgy director. Scorsese did his best to cover up the melodrama with honest performances and gritty location work – it still looks and feels right 30 years later. Unsure what to do with a woman's picture, Scorsese surrounded himself with women in the crew, and did improvisation to give the script more realism. The intimate scene between Burstyn and Kris Kristofferson, where Alice reveals her dreams, feels right because of this process. Ellen Burstyn won the Oscar for her performance and a TV series, called simply *Alice* (1976), was based around the diner.

Verdict: Whatever the 'feminist' or 'realistic' coating on this film, it is still a genre picture, a standard woman's melodrama circa 1950, where the poor woman struggles to make good and then a handsome rich guy comes along to domesticate woman and child. It was Burstyn and Scorsese's intention not to end the film with a movie ending, but Warner Brothers insisted and so the current compromise was filmed. A solid, slick piece of film-making. 3/5

Taxi Driver (1976)

Cast: Robert De Niro (Travis Bickle), Jodie Foster (Iris), Albert Brooks (Tom), Harvey Keitel (Sport), Leonard Harris (Charles Palantine), Peter Boyle (Wizard), Cybill Shepherd (Betsy), Norman Matlock (Charlie T), Diahnne Abbott (Concession Girl), Victor Argo (Deli Owner Melio), Harry Northup (Doughboy), Steven Prince (Andy, Gun Salesman), Joe Spinell (Personnel Officer)

Crew: Producers: Julia Phillips, Michael Phillips, Phillip M Goldfarb (Associate), Director: Martin Scorsese, Writer: Paul Schrader, Cinematographer: Michael Chapman, Supervising Editors: Marcia Lucas, Steven Spielberg (uncredited), Editors: Tom Rolf, Melvin Shapiro, Thelma Schoonmaker (uncredited), Composer: Bernard Herrmann, 113 mins

Story: Vietnam veteran Travis Bickle cannot sleep so he takes a job as a taxi driver. He tries to begin a relationship with beautiful Betsy, a political campaigner for presidential candidate Charles Palantine, but she rejects him after he takes her to a porn film on their first date. When Palantine gets into Travis' cab, Travis tells him that New York is an open sewer and that somebody should wash it all away. With bad thoughts in his head after Betsy rejects him, Travis buys guns and plans to assassinate Palantine as a vent for all his anger and frustration. Meanwhile, he tries to save 12-year-old Iris from a life of prostitution but she wants to stay with her pimp. The assassination attempt goes wrong and so Travis kills Iris' pimp in a bloody slaughter. Iris returns to her parents and Travis is hailed as a hero by the media.

Cine-Literate: Travis is cine-illiterate – he thinks it is romantic to take Betsy to a porn movie. Scorsese is more cine-literate in this area – when Travis is selecting the guns, he points one of them out the window and at people like a shot in Peter Bogdanovich's *Targets* (1967). (Bogdanovich and Cybill Shepherd were an item at the time.) The shot of Travis holding the Magnum revolver at arm's length emulates Clint Eastwood in *Dirty Harry* (Don Siegel, 1971) – by making this visual connection Scorsese reminds us that either Travis is a good guy, or that Harry is a villain, depending upon which way you view it. By making references to westerns (Travis in cowboy boots and Matthew/Sport (the pimp) looking like an Indian with his long hair and bandana) Scorsese points out the similarity to racist Ethan Edwards' search for his 'soiled' niece in *The Searchers* (John Ford, 1956). I also wonder if the scene where Travis tips and balances the TV with his feet (it eventually falls and smashes) was an echo of Henry Fonda's Wyatt Earp balancing on his chair in John Ford's *My Darling Clementine* (1946).

Home Movie: Martin is quite scary as Passenger Watching Silhouette (a last-minute part because the actor couldn't make it), but he also makes a cameo sitting outside the Palantine campaign HQ when Betsy is introduced. In a documentary, Jodie Foster commented that Scorsese had his parents on set for some of the shoot, and it was nice to see him interact with them. In the film,

Travis Bickle writes a card to his parents, and at the end Iris' parents write a thank you letter to Travis. Catherine and Charles are Iris' parents in the newspaper clipping hanging on Travis' wall at the end of the movie.

Picture: In conversation with Betsy, Travis mentions that he must get "organiz–ized" like the sign in offices. We later see this sign on the wall of his room, just before he goes out to buy guns as part of his assassination plan. The word pops up in his voice-over, a verbalisation of his notebooks: "June twenty-ninth. I gotta get in shape now. Too much sitting is ruining my body. Too much abuse is going on for too long. From now on there will be 50 push-ups each morning, 50 pull-ups. There will be no more pills, no more bad food, no more destroyers of my body. From now on it will be total organization. Every muscle must be tight."

Voice-Over: Obsessive people often write out all their ideas, as Travis does in his notebooks. These writings become the voice-over. He does not have a high level of education (as mentioned in his interview to become a taxi driver) and you can see this in his writing – upper and lower case letters are mixed within the same word.

Seeing: This is Scorsese's first film to fully integrate visual style and content. The film is shot mostly from Travis' point of view (a scene with Betsy in the Palantine campaign HQ and between Sport and Iris in the brothel are both outside of Travis' knowledge) so we follow him walking and driving down the mean streets. Significantly,

Travis is mostly in the frame on his own, and the taxi is mostly alone on the streets, or certainly the only vehicle fully in the frame, which echoes the theme of Travis' loneliness and apartness. As he says: "Loneliness has followed me my whole life, everywhere. In bars, in cars, sidewalks, stores, everywhere. There's no escape. I'm God's lonely man." The film is shot at different camera speeds to capture the internal speeds of the mind – Betsy's introduction is in romantic slow motion, as are Travis' bloodshot/drugged eyes in the mirror, yet the final slaughter is jagged/speeded up/slowed down like a machine breaking down. This is a journey through the mind's eye/notebooks of Travis Bickle.

Scorsese uses the overhead/God shot throughout the film: the taxi supervisor's desk; the food Travis buys at the porn theatre; the fizz of the tablet in the glass of water; Travis' hand over Betsy's desk; the guns that Travis wants to buy; the dead body after the hold-up; and finally after the slaughter.

Scorsese is so scary as Passenger Watching Silhouette that it is the only time in the film that we really feel that Travis is in danger. Travis is always seen from the front, and to one side, and he watches his passengers through the mirror. However, to give a hint of Travis' peril, Scorsese inserts a shot of the back of Travis' head (from the passenger's point of view), so that we can see how defenceless Travis really is. It is after this that Travis starts to get bad ideas in his head and decides to get a gun.

Hearing: The film score was written by Bernard Herrmann, who began his film career with *Citizen Kane*

PAUL DUNCAN

(1941) and became best known for his scores for Alfred
Hitchcock films like *Psycho* (1960), *North By Northwest*
(1959) and especially *Vertigo* (1958). *Vertigo*, a film about
obsession and madness, most closely resembles *Taxi Driver*,
which was Herrmann's last film. The horrible thoughts
and actions of James Stewart in *Vertigo* are made acceptable
because of the romantic/foreboding score. Similarly,
Herrmann evokes the romantic/foreboding side of Travis
Bickle. He thinks he is a knight in shining armour, but he
is instead being devoured by the demons within.

Subtext: Obsession – Travis' repulsion of New York is
understandable because he sees the worst of people in the
back of his cab. What kind of world is it where he has to
wipe the cum and blood off the back seat at the end of
every shift? The people he meets are abusive, violent and
psychopathic. He is disgusted by this world. He fought in
Vietnam, in the Marines, and returned to a horrible world.
Mirror Scene – The famous "You talking to me?" mirror
scene where Travis practises how he will react when
confronted is funny and horrifying at the same time. The
film is full of mirror scenes, because Travis talks to people
through his rear-view mirror in the cab. As in Hitchcock's
Rear Window (1954), Travis is trapped in his environment,
views the world through his window (and mirror) and
makes judgements on it. Although Travis' status as a
Vietnam veteran is not overstated, the psychology and
mannerisms of a vet seem very well observed. It makes
sense that a man who had to watch his back in 'Nam
would feel that he needs to do so in New York also –
hence the window and rear-view mirror allow him to

keep an eye out for danger at all times. (Also, this tension/alertness to danger results in sleeplessness.) It strikes me that such a man, shocked by the war, would feel alienated from the world and disgusted by it but at the same time wants to be part of it. He would also be full of self-hate because of his past actions. The rear-view mirror then becomes the eyes to his soul. In the final scene, when we see those horrible red eyes (his demons) in the rear-view mirror, we know that Travis' loneliness is not at an end and that he will lead a Jekyll & Hyde existence. Travis has not changed, and neither will Iris and the other characters. Religion – Travis is searching for redemption from his guilt/evil thoughts through a cathartic act. He is trying to kill the father (Palantine) of the virgin (Betsy) but when that fails he kills the father (Sport) of the whore (Iris). As in *Who's That Knocking At My Door?* and *Mean Streets*, the virgin/whore vision of women still exists. These religious themes return more seriously in *The Last Temptation Of Christ*, and melodramatically in *Cape Fear*.

Background: *Taxi Driver* was written by Paul Schrader in 10 days after a period when he was living in a car following the break-up of a relationship. He realised that he hadn't spoken to anybody for days and the taxi became a metaphor for loneliness. Schrader, a former film critic, had sold his script for *The Yakuza* (Sydney Pollack, 1974) for a very large sum of money but no studio would take on the bleak (but great) script for *Taxi Driver*. Scorsese wanted it, but had to wait until he had a track record and could secure De Niro (hot from *The Godfather II*), before getting a budget. In preparation De Niro drove taxis in

New York on the weekend, whilst filming *1900* (Bernardo Bertolucci, 1976) in Italy during the week. Schrader found a girl prostitute to use as the basis for Iris, and her mannerisms (eating sugar and jam on bread, different coloured sunglasses) were used by Jodie Foster – the girl appears as Iris' friend in the film. Harvey Keitel researched pimps and added a long nail on his little finger when he found out cocaine addicts used them as scoops. Again, scenes between De Niro and Keitel were improvised and then incorporated into the script before filming. Each addition from cast and crew added a layer to the original script rather than revise it. For example, when Travis watches a pop show on TV, the script emphasises the grinding, lusty bodies – the sex-flesh that Travis lusts for but cannot have. Scorsese has this in the film, but the song they are dancing to contains the words "close to the end" and "how long have I been sleeping?" which gives a premonition of bad things to come. The production took over a condemned building to film Travis' room, Iris' room and the final shoot-out. The overhead shot at the end was achieved by cutting a long hole through the ceiling – it weakened the structure of the building so much that the crew feared for their safety. There was so much blood on the walls that it looked and smelt like an abattoir. However, this pungent red was desaturated in order to get an R rating. Although this red is now lost forever (the negative colour is not recoverable) the desaturation gives the effect of a nightmare and something happening inside the mind, which is appropriate.

Taxi Driver struck a chord with many people, echoing Thomas Wolfe's observation that loneliness is the 'central and inevitable fact of human existence.' John Hinckley went so far as to re-enact the film by attempting to assassinate Ronald Reagan in 1981 to prove his obsessive love to Jodie Foster. Sadly some people blamed the film, without realising it was merely mirroring society.

Verdict: Undoubtedly, Scorsese's first masterpiece, but also the result of a tight collaboration between Scorsese, De Niro, Schrader, Herrmann and cinematographer Michael Chapman. 5/5

New York, New York (1977)

Cast: Liza Minnelli (Francine Evans), Robert De Niro (Jimmy Doyle), Lionel Stander (Tony Harwell), Barry Primus (Paul Wilson), Mary Kay Place (Bernice), Georgie Auld (Frankie Harte), George Memmoli (Nicky), Dick Miller (Palm Club Owner), Murray Moston (Horace Morris), Lenny Gaines (Artie Kirks), Clarence Clemons (Cecil Powell), Kathi McGinnis (Ellen Flannery), Adam David Winkler (Jimmy Doyle Jr), Frank Sivera (Eddie Di Muzio), Diahnne Abbott (Harlem Club Singer), Margo Winkler (Argumentative Woman), Steven Prince (Record Producer), Casey Kasem (DJ), Harry Northup (Alabama), Mardik Martin (Well Wisher in Moonlit Terrace)

Crew: Director: Martin Scorsese, Writers: Earl Mac Rauch, Mardik Martin, Story: Earl Mac Rauch, Producers: Irwin Winkler, Robert Chartoff, Gene Kirkwood (Associate), Cinematographer: László Kovács, Supervising Editor: Marcia Lucas, Editors: Bert Lovitt,

David Ramirez, Tom Rolf, Songs: Fred Ebb, John Kander, 164 mins

Story: On VJ Day 1945 in New York, fast-talking ex-soldier Jimmy Doyle tries to pick up women to have a bit of fun but all he gets is "No!" He fixates on and is attracted to quiet, sensible Francine Evans. When they find out that he is a jazzed-up saxophone player and she a singer with the Frankie Harte band, their attraction grows because they make a "Major Chord" when they are together according to Jimmy. They marry but life on the road with Frankie Harte does not suit Jimmy because it stifles his creativity, and he does not have the temperament for big band music. He is also insanely jealous of Francine's success. They split up when Francine has their baby – Jimmy to pursue his jazz/drugs and Francine her singing/family. Years later they meet up when both have been successful in their chosen careers. There is an opportunity for them to get together again, but they don't.

Cine-Literate: Scorsese based the film on the noir musical *The Man I Love* (Raoul Walsh, 1946). Francine sings 'The Man I Love' at an audition – she sings to the same actor who auditioned Alice in *Alice Doesn't Live Here Any More*. When Jimmy watches a sailor and blonde (Liza Minnelli in wig) dancing without music, it is a reference to *On The Town* (Stanley Donen/Gene Kelly, 1949), which features the city and song 'New York, New York.' Jimmy signs into a hotel as 'Michael Powell,' Scorsese's favourite director. Liza Minnelli is the daughter of Vincente Minnelli and Judy Garland – the storyline echoes

Garland's *A Star Is Born* (George Cukor, 1954) whilst the visual style echoes Vincente Minnelli's musicals.

Home Movie: Even though *New York, New York* was supposed to be a genre movie, there are uncomfortable parallels between it and Scorsese's life. Jimmy's struggle between home life and career (cf. *Alice Doesn't Live Here Any More*) reflects Scorsese's own problems. Jimmy's drug problem – merely alluded to rather than shown – reflected Scorsese's drug use. Taking drugs to stay awake for all night editing sessions was common practice, but at some stage in the early 1970s the Hollywood community moved from soft to hard drugs. Scorsese was part of this lifestyle.

Picture: During Jimmy's audition you can see a large picture behind him of George Washington on his horse. In a motel room a reproduction of the *Mona Lisa* hangs on the wall.

Seeing: Lots of swooping camera à la Vincente Minnelli. Lots of overhead shots when Jimmy stands up and blows his sax at the heavens. Lots of lovely stylised sets courtesy of veteran Boris Leven (*Giant* (1956), *West Side Story* (1961) and a million other stylish films you've seen). The whole film is colourful. There is one scene set in a blood red club. Jimmy wears an orange suit! Time elapsing is shown whilst one song is being sung. When Jimmy returns to a pregnant Francine, and later when Jimmy visits the successful Franci e, she first spies him through a mirror. There is one lor *g* close-up of Francine's eyes.

Hearing: Ladies and gentlemen, let us give praise to George Auld's delightful sax playing. George, take a bow. And Liza . . . you did good too.

Subtext: Francine and Jimmy are two creative people who are in love, but they are totally unsuited to each other. This story is at odds with the usual happy ending of such musicals. Ironically, Scorsese comments on this expectation in a 12-minute film-within-the-film called *Happy Endings*, which is a traditional Hollywood musical circa 1950. A great sequence (sarcastically called *Sappy Endings* by Jimmy Doyle), it follows in the footsteps of the ballet sequences in Powell and Pressburger's *The Red Shoes* (1948) and in *An American In Paris* (Vincente Minnelli, 1951).

Francine represents the nice girl singer who often fronted big bands in the 1940s. The film follows her evolution into a singer who adds the weight of her broken heart to her performance. She begins the film quiet and ends it loud and passionate. Her most affecting performance is her rendition of 'New York, New York' at the end. Jimmy, on the other hand, is a jazz saxophonist who jumps and screeches (he's great in the Harlem club) but who ends up mellow and low key, successfully running his club, The Major Chord. He starts loud and ends up quiet.

In the end both characters are being true to their talents and to themselves. Jimmy is honest with Francine and tells her at the beginning that he is only interested in music, money and women, and that if she went with him, he would move her up the list.

Background: On the back of *Taxi Driver*'s Palme D'Or at Cannes and De Niro's great reviews, the lads got a bit cocky on the set of *New York, New York*. Given a weak script and being forced to shoot because Liza Minnelli had a Las Vegas contract to fulfil, Scorsese directed his actors to improvise scenes, and drew out quite gritty/painful performances. However, it was all very last-minute and focussed on the scene at hand rather than at the film as a whole. Consequently the performances are at odds with the smooth big band-era visual style that Scorsese had adopted. In love with the films of Vincente Minnelli and George Cukor, and getting the great Boris Leven to do the studio sets, the film looks like a 1950s MGM musical but the actors are performing in a John Cassevetes movie. The film just doesn't gel.

Verdict: *New York, New York* commits the cardinal sin of being interesting in parts but boring overall. 2/5

The Last Waltz (1978)

Cast: Robbie Robertson, Rick Danko, Levon Helm, Garth Hudson, Richard Manuel, Dr John, Ringo Starr, Muddy Waters, Ron Wood, Neil Young, Paul Butterfield, Eric Clapton, Neil Diamond, Bob Dylan, Emmylou Harris, Ronnie Hawkins, Joni Mitchell, Van Morrison, Roebuck 'Pops' Staples, Martin Scorsese (Interviewer)

Crew: Director: Martin Scorsese, Cinematographers: Michael Chapman, Michael W Watkins, Vilmos Zsigmond, László Kovács, Producers: Robbie Robertson, LA Johnson

(Line), Frank Marshall (Line), Steven Prince (Associate), Jonathan T Taplin (Executive), Joel Chernoff (Uncredited), 117 mins

Story: After 16 years on the road, The Band decided to play their final gig on Thanksgiving 1976 at the Winterland in San Francisco, where they played their first gig. They invited friends and people who influenced them, hence the impressive line-up of guests from every type of musical style. Scorsese starts with the last song, intermingles interviews with The Band, and includes three songs filmed on an MGM soundstage.

Home Movie: Martin did all the interviews.

Picture: There is a photo of the New York skyline in the background of one of the interviews.

Moral: The road was "A goddamned impossible way of life" according to Robbie Robertson.

Seeing: We start with Rick Danko playing pool at The Band's recording studio, Shangri-La, which used to be a bordello. This is the seedy/tacky background for the interviews. Rick Danko looks like Johnny Boy from *Mean Streets* – they all look like background characters from Scorsese's movies. The three songs shot on the MGM soundstage use a swooping camera. The final song is done in one take, from close-up on an instrument, across the players and finally up and out far away – a sort of reverse of Hitchcock's famous shot at the end of *Young And Innocent* (1937).

Subtext: As well as the love of music communicated at the concert, the film tells the story of The Band on the road and how each song relates to them, and also the story of the fusions that make rock and roll music. Of particular interest are 'The Weight' which is a song about the transference of guilt.

Background: Six weeks before the concert, The Band decided to film it and asked Scorsese because of his previous use of music in his films and his experience editing music films (*Woodstock* (1970), *Medicine Ball Caravan* (1971) and *Elvis On Tour* (1972)). Scorsese had just finished a 100-day shoot on *New York, New York* and took some time off editing to film the concert. He brought in Boris Leven to do the set, and some of the best cinematographers to operate the cameras.

Verdict: An excellent concert film that captures the emotion of the music and the night. 4/5

American Boy: A Profile Of Steven Prince (1978)

Cast: Steven Prince, George Memmoli, Martin Scorsese

Crew: Director: Martin Scorsese, Producers: Bert Lovitt, Jim Wheat (Executive), Ken Wheat (Executive), Cinematographer: Michael Chapman, Editors: Amy Holden Jones, Bert Lovitt, Composer: Neil Young, 55 mins

Story: Prince tells amusing and horrifying stories about growing up (home movies act as point and counterpoint), being Neil Diamond's road manager, getting into drugs and guns, and that sort of thing. Prince looks as though he is high on drugs throughout the whole film.

Moral: Steven Prince: "I'm a survivor."

Background: This TV documentary was filmed for $155,000 in George Memmoli's house, and can be seen as a sort of coda to *Taxi Driver*. Indeed, Prince played Easy Andy (the gun and drug dealer) in *Taxi Driver*. However, what is more interesting is Prince's omnipresence in Scorsese's life during this period as Scorsese's assistant and personal bodyguard. There is a hint of this relationship in Peter Biskind's book *Easy Riders, Raging Bulls* but it has never been fully explored.

Verdict: Prince is a natural storyteller and you cannot help but be sucked into his worldview, and to laugh with everybody else. But ultimately, he takes us to dark places we would rather not visit, where humour turns to black humour and then to darkness. After he tells the story of how he blew away a mad Indian at a deserted gas station, and put six rounds into him, Prince explains that his father, an Army man, always taught him that when you shot a guy you made sure he never got up again. "The experience of killing a man . . ." Prince leaves the thought unfinished. It wouldn't surprise me if the character of Tommy DeVito (Joe Pesci) in *GoodFellas* was partly based on Prince. (And I wonder if Johnny Boy in *Mean Streets* was partly based on Prince.) Towards the end, when Prince says, "I'm happy," his eyes say something else. In retrospect, this is an incredibly sad film. 4/5

Raging Bull (1980)

Cast: Robert De Niro (Jake La Motta), Cathy Moriarty (Vickie La Motta), Joe Pesci (Joey La Motta), Frank Vincent (Salvy), Nicholas Colasanto (Tommy Como), Theresa Saldana (Lenore), Mario Gallo (Mario), Frank Adonis (Patsy), Joseph Bono (Guido), Frank Topham (Toppy), Lori Anne Flax (Irma), Don Dunphy (Himself/Radio Announcer), Bernie Allen (Comedian), Johnny Barnes (Sugar Ray Robinson), Kevin Mahon (Tony Janiro), Eddie Mustafa Muhammad (Billy Fox), Louis Raftis (Marcel Cerdan), Coley Wallace (Joe Louis), Johnny Turner (Laurent Dauthuille), Peter Fain (Dauthuille Corner Man), Ted Husing (Himself), Mardik Martin (Copa Waiter), Peter Savage (Jackie Curtie), John Turturro (Man at Table)

Crew: Director: Martin Scorsese, Writers: Paul Schrader, Mardik Martin, Book: Jake La Motta, Joseph Carter, Peter Savage, Producers: Irwin Winkler, Robert Chartoff, Hal W Polaire (Associate), Peter Savage (Associate), Cinematographer: Michael Chapman, Editor: Thelma Schoonmaker, Composers: Pietro Mascagni (from *Cavalleria Rusticana*), Robbie Robertson, Consultant: Jake La Motta, Technical Advisors: Al Silvani, Frank Topham, 129 mins, B&W

Story: Beginning in New York City, 1964, we hear a bloated Jake La Motta practice his lounge act on a boxing theme. Included are film and literary quotes with a few jokes thrown in for good measure. We jump back to 1941 and follow the events of Jake's boxing and personal life.

There are several story threads. Jake is reluctant to be managed by Tommy Como, who is connected, but Jake cannot get a title fight so throws a fight and two years later wins the title. In this thread there is a sense that Jake has sinned, that he is no longer pure after Tommy becomes his manager. The next thread is his relationship with Vicki, who becomes his wife. Jake is insanely jealous. His possessive/controlling nature means that he can never be happy with her. Lastly, there is Jake's relationship with his brother, Joey, who is also his manager. Whereas Jake wants to do things the right way, Joey is more practical and wise to the ways of the world. Jake and Joey fool around, have fun and argue like brothers. However, Jake's attitude towards his wife and brother turns abusive and violent, leading to an irrevocable split with them. This attitude seems to stem from Jake's self-loathing after throwing a fight and accepting Tommy Como's connections. Jake's victories are bittersweet and become meaningless. Returning to 1964, Jake quotes Marlon Brando's "I coulda been a contender" speech, when he bemoans his betrayal by his brother. From this we come to understand that Jake feels he was betrayed by his brother, and their brief meeting at the end is Jake's unspoken forgiveness and, at the same time, apology for what happened between them.

Wiseguy: Tommy Como is the godfather, a lovely old man who is nice to everybody and sorts out problems, much like Giovanni in *Mean Streets*. Salvy works for Tommy and talks to Joey, so that they can persuade Jake to fight for Tommy. Salvy is an object of hate for Jake, not just because he is a wiseguy (he gets money in a dishonourable way) but he also goes on dates with Vicki (jealousy). Jake is presented as a working-class hero compared to the elegant and coiffured wiseguys.

Cine-Literate: *On The Waterfront* (Elia Kazan, 1954) is quoted by Jake at the end. *Raging Bull* owes a lot to boxing movies like *Body And Soul* (Robert Rossen, 1947) and *The Set-Up* (Robert Wise, 1948), but it reminds me most of the noirish *Champion* (Mark Robson, 1949), an ugly story of a man who will stop at nothing to get to the top. Magnificently played by Kirk Douglas, the final fight where his beaten and horribly distorted face breathes like an animal (thus showing the inner animal of the character) is truly shocking. Scorsese has said that he and De Niro liked watching *Force Of Evil* (Abraham Polonsky, 1948), a fabulous Film Noir about the numbers racket, because of the complex relationship between the brothers.

Home Movie: Charles is one of the mob wiseguys (called 'Charlie') who pops up several times as a friend of Tommy Como. Martin Scorsese plays the (unseen) Barbizon stage-hand who asks Jake to go on stage at the end.

Picture: There are religious pictures on the wall when Jake takes Vicki home.

Moral: 'Once I was blind, and now I can see.'

Seeing: The complexity of the roving camera, lighting and staging in this film is worth a book of its own. This is probably Scorsese's most fully realised and executed film, with every shot revealing inner character. The film is bookended by 'fat' Jake looking in the mirror in the dressing room, implying that the film are his thoughts and perhaps his acknowledgement of the horror inside him. Is he trying to make sense of it? Certainly the expressionistic camerawork gives the impression that everything is distorted and heightened, like in memories. As in *Mean Streets*, Scorsese uses home movies within the frame, this time of Jake and Joey marrying, having children and living a life. Ironically, the home movies are presented as faded colour whilst the film is in black and white. We remember in black and white, don't we?

Sound: There is a great long tracking shot from the dressing room, through the corridors, up through the crowd and then into the ring. What makes this so effective is both the sad classical music overlaying it (Mascagini) and the changes in sound levels and types. The popping camera bulbs are like bullets (they are actually gunshots), the sounds of animals overlay the breathing of the fighters (tigers and bulls), then a deafening silence before the sickening crunches of the blows (melons and tomatoes being squashed).

The sounds and images are conducted throughout the film, so that the scenes at home are often flat/static in a neorealist style, whilst the scenes in the ring are full of music/sound/movement/emotion. The ring is the dream place where Jake is most alive and honest.

Subtext: There is a Spanish scene in Orson Welles' *Mr Arkadin* when a woman asks about a religious procession where people are flagellating themselves. She is told they are penitents. "They must be awful sorry," she observes. The beating that Jake La Motta takes in the ring, and gives himself in his jail cell, is his self-punishment for all the wrong things he does. Jake is an unfettered brute, wracked with jealousy and frustration. There is something inside him that fuels his self-destruction.

As with *Taxi Driver*, we do not have an analysis or explanation of the central character, but we see the results of Jake's psychology. Unlike *Taxi Driver*, we see the transformation, or self-realisation of Jake La Motta, who eventually sees what a horrible person he had been.

Jake tells Joey near the beginning that his hands are too small which means that he will never be able to fight Joe Louis, the best fighter in the world. Jake's ambition to prove that he is the best in the world can never be achieved. Furthermore, his love of the sport is pure as shown by his resistance to being managed by Tommy and his wiseguys. (Jake knows he is living in a corrupt society, but does not want to be trapped by it.) Eventually, Jake understands that Tommy must manage him if Jake is to get a shot at the title, but this comes at a terrible price – throwing a fight. After this, Jake's spirit becomes sick, so that even winning the title fight (with Joe Louis congratulating him) cannot compensate for the dishonour he has had to endure. The tears of victory are also tears of spiritual defeat.

Scorsese films Jake winning the title fight with sad music overpowering the ambient sound. This shows the interior sadness of Jake. Indeed, each of the fights are filmed in a different style to reflect Jake's interior

emotions. When he is beaten·to a pulp by Sugar Ray
Robinson (the implication is that Jake is allowing this to
happen as self-punishment for the beating he has given his
brother Joey, and the slapping he gave Vicky), Jake is in the
pit of Hell. Scorsese shows this by putting flames under
the camera so that there is a heat shimmer on the image.

In the beginning, Jake is very suspicious of everybody
around him, except his brother Joey. He is suspicious of
the wiseguys, especially Salvy, who is trying to sign up Jake
with Tommy, and who is going out on dates with Vicky.
When Jake marries Vicky, he becomes suspicious of her
when she says another boxer is good looking. (Jake beats
the boxer to a pulp and later tells Vicky he ain't so good
looking now.) After he reluctantly signs up with Tommy,
Jake begins to suspect Joey of having an affair with Vicky.
The tension within Jake eventually explodes because Jake
has got the world title (in a way he thinks is dishonourable) and has no more goals to achieve. He has no
outlet for the violence inside him other than to direct it at
his family. It has all gone bad.

At the end, when Jake recites Marlon Brando's famous
speech from *On The Waterfront*, when Brando says to his
brother Rod Steiger, "You, you were my brother, you
shoulda looked out for me," Jake is similarly lamenting that
his brother Joey should have acted in his best interests,
instead of making him sell out and throw a fight. Jake is
also talking to himself in the mirror, and this scene shows
us that Jake has attained a degree of self-realisation. Jake
now understands that he was an animal who brutalised the
people he loved. The brief, awkward scene where Jake sees
and embraces Joey after many years, shows a degree of

affection and regret that had been missing previously. Scorsese underlines this self-revelation by ending the film with the Biblical quote, 'once I was blind, and now I can see.'

Background: Robert De Niro trained for a year to become fit and get the right mentality for the role. After boxing over 1000 rounds, he entered in three genuine Brooklyn boxing matches and won two of them. After filming his 'thin' sequences, the production broke for four months while De Niro put on 60 pounds to play in the 'fat' sequences. Scorsese and De Niro had seen Joe Pesci in low-budget film *The Death Collector* (1975) and wanted him for the part of Joey, so they tracked him down. Pesci had mainly worked as a musician, singing and playing guitar, but after *Raging Bull*, he appeared in the *Home Alone* and *Lethal Weapon* franchises.

Verdict: 5/5

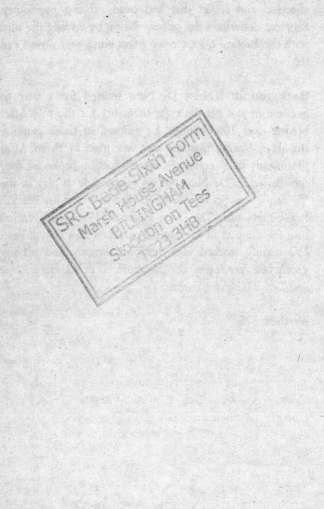
SRC Bede Sixth Form
Marsh House Avenue
BILLINGHAM
Stockton on Tees
TS23 3HB

3 Out On A Limb

The King Of Comedy (1983)

Cast: Robert De Niro (Rupert Pupkin), Jerry Lewis (Jerry Langford), Diahnne Abbott (Rita), Sandra Bernhard (Masha), Ed Herlihy (Himself), Liza Minnelli (Herself), Dr Joyce Brothers (Herself), Victor Borge (Himself), Tony Randall (Himself), Margo Winkler (Receptionist), Shelley Hack (Cathy Long), Mick Jones (Street Scum), Joe Strummer (Street Scum), Paul Simonon (Street Scum), Don Letts (Street Scum), Peter Fain (Plain clothes man), Mardik Martin (Second Man at Bar), Mary Elizabeth Mastrantonio (Scenes Deleted)

Crew: Director: Martin Scorsese, Writer: Paul D Zimmermann, Producers: Arnon Milchan, Robert F Colesberry (Associate), Robert Greenhut (Executive), Cinematographer: Fred Schuler, Editor: Thelma Schoonmaker, Composer: Robbie Robertson, Steadicam Operator: Garrett Brown, 101 mins

Story: Would-be stand up comedian Rupert Pupkin seems to be a fan of talk show host Jerry Langford. However, all he wants is a meeting with Jerry, to get a comedy spot on the show. Rupert records a tape of his 'appearance' in his basement room, which is furnished as a talk show set. There is even a cardboard cut-out of Jerry hanging on Rupert's every word. Rupert imagines getting married on the show, with his High School principal apologising about the school's previous attitude towards Rupert and begging his forgiveness. After his tape is rejected and he is thrown out of Jerry's production office, Rupert turns up at Jerry's house, pretending that he and Jerry are good friends, in order to impress new girlfriend Rita. Unable to take no for an answer, Rupert and Jerry fan Masha, kidnap Jerry. Rupert demands that he appear on the show and that it is broadcast before Jerry is released. Masha's fantasy of a night alone with Jerry is also fulfilled. That evening, Rupert shows Rita his appearance on TV and he is arrested. He becomes rich and famous and achieves his dream.

Cine-Literate: There is a clip from *Pickup On South Street* (Samuel Fuller, 1953), a film about two outsiders, a prostitute and a pickpocket, who team up to defeat the Red Menace.

Home Movie: There is a great, improvised scene with Catherine Scorsese, who plays Rupert's Mom off-camera as he is trying to record his audition tape. She shouts down for him to lower the sound each time he is setting the tape to record. The timing is perfect and De Niro broke down laughing on the set. Charles plays a man at the bar and Martin has a cameo as a TV director.

Picture: When Rupert is practising his routine, he is shown in front of a large picture of an audience. We can hardly hear him, but we can hear the laughter. This is one of several 'daydreams' that appear throughout the film.

Moral: Rupert Pupkin: "Better to be king for a night than a schmuck for a lifetime."

Seeing: Everything is mundane, muted, flat and natural.

Hearing: The script is littered with false words and sounds, so that you do not hear what you expect to hear. When a secretary asks Rupert if Mr Langford is expecting him, Rupert replies, "Yes, I don't think he is." When Rupert is recording his audition tape, his preamble includes the classic line, "I know, Jerry, that you are as human as the rest of us, if not more so." The canned laughter in this sequence means that he is forcing the audience to laugh at him, just as he forces people to watch him. In the end, the irony is that people like his jokes.

Subtext: Like *Raging Bull*, *The King Of Comedy* is about the desire to succeed at any price. However, the difference is that Rupert is without self-loathing. He is a sociopath, who is only concerned with his own well-being and will stop at nothing to achieve his ambition. Like Jake La Motta, he is good at what he does, and when Rupert gets his 'title shot' he wins. The media generates people like Rupert to want celebrity at any price. We live in a world where people are famous for being famous, a world that Scorsese satirizes here to great effect. (Compare this to the end of *Taxi Driver*, where Travis is lauded as a hero, but the truth is different.) We live in a corrupt world.

Although Rupert dresses and acts like a nerd, and seems polite enough, there is an underlying toughness and violence to him that is unnerving. He steadfastly refuses to accept any other person's point of view, which leads to tensions. The scene where Rupert and Rita go to visit Jerry's house is a masterpiece of sustained underlying anger. Rupert is jealous of Jerry and all he has achieved, and is also angry with Jerry, even though he must also respect him. These conflicting feelings are ones that most people in the entertainment business must deal with as they go up and down the celebrity charts.

Background: After the great critical success of *Raging Bull*, with all its method acting and swooping camera movements (the 'look at me' school of film-making), Scorsese and De Niro switched gears to make a very flat/opaque film with more naturalistic acting and invisible camerawork. The result was a terrible box-office flop ($20 million to make, with gross returns of $2.5 million in the US) and made it difficult for Scorsese to continue with personal projects. The high cost was partly due to the extensive New York locations, and partly due to the improvisation that led to up to 40 takes of each scene. (Jerry Lewis found it difficult to adapt to some of these practices but he eventually got into it.)

Verdict: 5/5

After Hours (1985)

Cast: Griffin Dunne (Paul Hackett), Rosanna Arquette (Marcy), Verna Bloom (June), Tommy Chong (Pepe), Linda Fiorentino (Kiki), Teri Garr (Julie), John Heard (Tom the Bartender), Cheech Marin (Neil), Catherine O'Hara (Gail), Dick Miller (Waiter), Will Patton (Horst), Larry Block (Taxi Driver), Victor Argo (Diner Cashier), Margo Winkler (Woman with Gun), Rockets Redglare (Angry Mob Member)

Crew: Director: Martin Scorsese, Writer: Joseph Minion, Producers: Robert F Colesberry, Griffin Dunne, Amy Robinson, Deborah Schindler (Associate), Cinematographer: Michael Ballhaus, Editor: Thelma Schoonmaker, Composer: Howard Shore, 96 mins

Story: Paul is an office worker. Restless after work, he meets Marcy at a coffee shop and then calls her up later that night, hoping to meet and sleep with her. However, going downtown to SoHo proves to be dangerous. He loses his last $20 bill out the window of the taxi. Marcy is depressed after breaking up with her boyfriend and commits suicide. Her flatmate Kiki is a sculptress into S&M. There are burglars on the prowl. Eventually Paul is accused of being the burglar and is chased around SoHo. He escapes by being made into a sculpture and ends up at his office the following morning as the doors are being opened.

Cine-Literate: Marcy tells Paul that her husband was obsessed by *The Wizard Of Oz* (1939) and that when he reached climax during lovemaking he would shout out, "Surrender Dorothy!"

Home Movie: Martin Scorsese appears in Club Berlin operating a searchlight. Catherine Scorsese was a production assistant and Charles Scorsese was a wardrobe assistant as well as appearing on screen.

Moral: Different rules apply when it's after hours.

Seeing: Scorsese returns to his highly stylised swooping camera and quick cut style. This style is appropriate for a dreamlike tale where people and events rush by. It is a more comedic version of Orson Welles' *The Trial* (1963), based on Franz Kafka's novel, which follows Josef K's search for justice in an unfair and uncaring world. In fact, in one scene of *After Hours* a bouncer refuses Paul entry into Club Berlin and the dialogue is a direct lift from Kakfa's short story 'At The Door Of The Law,' which prefaces Welles' film.

We see the world from Paul's point of view throughout. When Kiki drops her keys from the window, they come straight down at us/Paul and we wince as he does. Paul is afraid of burns and he is shocked to see burns on Marcy's inner thigh. This mark is later revealed to be a tattoo that looks nothing like burns – Paul's mind has distorted what he sees. This odyssey of misdirection is a key element of 'all night' movies like *Into The Night* (1985).

Hearing: This black comedy has some great dialogue, especially the lines between Paul and Marcy.

Subtext: At the beginning of the film, self-absorbed Paul Hackett is content with the work that he does as a word processor. This is confirmed by the classical music that is heard whilst he is in this environment. At the end of the film he returns to work and classical music is heard again, for the first time since he left. This gives the impression that his work place is where he is most comfortable. When he travels to SoHo, where all the artists are, he feels he is in danger. Artists are a danger to society, are they not? His night odyssey in search of a woman/sex results in him meeting a variety of women, none of whom he is comfortable with. It is much safer for him to be away from artists, from women, at work.

This tension between artists and non-artists is a theme in many Scorsese pictures. The cop who holds Rupert in *The King Of Comedy* does not like Rupert's jokes. Similarly, when burglars Pepe and Neil steal a sculpture (actually Paul encased in papier mâché) Neil says: "The uglier the art, the more it's worth." Pepe replies: "This must be worth a fortune, man."

Background: After the big-budget box-office failures of *New York, New York* and *The King Of Comedy*, Scorsese had spent most of 1983 trying to get *The Last Temptation of Christ* made, but it all fell through four weeks before filming because the executives did not want to start a controversy. Trying to recover from this, he got back into psychological shape with the lean independent production *After Hours*. (Perhaps Scorsese felt that a comedy about a man for whom everything goes wrong reflected his recent dealings with Hollywood.) Working on a budget of $4.5

million, Scorsese shot at night with German cinematographer Michael Ballhaus, who had worked with Rainer Werner Fassbinder. Ballhaus worked so quickly, Scorsese didn't have to go back to his trailer to wait for lights to be set. The film was shot and edited, but nobody could come up with a satisfactory ending. It was suggested that June, the mother figure, grow larger and that Paul returns to her womb, but executive David Geffen found that outrageous. Eventually, upon the suggestion of Michael Powell, the current ending was shot and added in. The film went on to bank over $10 million and Scorsese received the Palme d'Or for Best Director at Cannes.

Verdict: Another black comedy from Scorsese, and a comedy that's actually funny. 4/5

'Mirror Mirror' in Amazing Stories (1986)

Cast: Sam Waterston (Jordan Mann), Helen Shaver (Karen), Dick Cavett (Himself), Tim Robbins (Jordan's Phantom), Harry Northup (Security Guard)

Crew: Director: Martin Scorsese, Story: Steven Spielberg, Teleplay: Joseph Minion, 24 mins

Story: Jordan Mann is a horror novelist who says he does not get scared, and then begins to see a phantom in mirrors. Each time he sees the phantom it gets closer and closer, yet when he turns around there is nothing there. Jordan begins to fall apart and is comforted by his girlfriend Karen. As they kiss, he sees the phantom reflected in her eyes and it strangles him. Jordan is transformed into the phantom and jumps out of the window.

Cine-Literate: There is a clip of *The Plague Of The Zombies* (John Gilling, 1966) at the beginning, purporting to be a film version of one of Jordan Mann's stories. The phantom looks a bit like The Phantom Of The Opera with a hat.

Picture: There are large reproductions of Jordan's book covers on his wall. The titles are *Eyes Of Terror*, *The Killer's Hand* and *Screen Dreams*. Appropriate for the story, don't you think?

Moral: Jordan Mann to Dick Cavett: "The whole point is to disturb and excite people."

Seeing: You can't really expect stylistic flourishes on such a tight shoot, but Scorsese includes a slow-motion shot of steam on an orange light (shades of *Taxi Driver*) and there are a lot of whip pans as Jordan looks behind him. This is the mirror scene to end all mirror scenes.

Subtext: After his interview with Dick Cavett, Jordan is riding home in a limousine and tells the driver that he is not afraid of ghosts, that he is more afraid of real things like agents and ex-wives. He is proved wrong. Pretty simple really.

Background: Scorsese filmed this in six days with no final cut. It was aired on the 9 March 1986 as Episode 19 of *Amazing Stories*.

Verdict: Nothing to write home about, but it does continue Scorsese's desire to direct different genres. After the musical (*New York, New York*), he did horror ('Mirror, Mirror'), before doing a film noir thriller (*Cape Fear*). 2/5

The Color Of Money (1986)

Cast: Paul Newman ('Fast' Eddie Felson), Tom Cruise (Vincent), Mary Elizabeth Mastrantonio (Carmen), Helen Shaver (Janelle), John Turturro (Julian), Bill Cobbs (Orvis)

Crew: Director: Martin Scorsese, Writer: Richard Price, Book: Walter Tevis, Producers: Irving Axelrod, Barbara De Fina, Dodie Foster (Associate), Cinematographer: Michael Ballhaus, Editor: Thelma Schoonmaker, Composer: Robbie Robertson, 117 mins

Story: Twenty or so years after being forced to quit playing pool in *The Hustler* (Robert Rossen, 1961), liquor salesman Eddie Felson decides to act as stake horse to Vincent, a naïve but incredibly talented player. Carmen is the only one who can control Vincent, so the three go on the road to tighten their game for the Atlantic City tournament. Their game is hustling as much money out of people as possible, but Vincent is too intent on winning to be very successful. Meanwhile, watching Vincent's natural ability draws Eddie back onto the pool table. Having taught Vincent and Carmen all he knows (because Carmen too must learn how to hustle), Eddie cuts loose and teaches himself how to play again. At the tournament, Eddie and Vincent play each other and Eddie wins. But

Eddie gets a rude awakening – Vincent had dumped the game to win a pile of money and presents Eddie with an envelope full of cash. Realising that he has created a monster, Eddie wants to play Vincent again and again, until he beats him. "I'm back!" Eddie declares emphatically at the end. Cue music and end titles.

Cine-Literate: There is a poster for *Carmen* (Francesco Rosi, 1984) in the room that Carmen and Vincent leave to go on the road. Carmen, of course played with two men, and there is a hint of this triangular relationship in Scorsese's movie. Iggy Pop, who has a cameo as a pool player, wears an *Attack Of The 50 Foot Woman* (1958) T-shirt.

Home Movie/Voice-Over: Martin does the voice-over at the beginning, and is seen in the Atlantic City casino walking his dog Zoe. Charlie has a bit part as a high roller.

Picture: There are paintings of nude women at the Atlantic City hotel bar where Eddie meets Vincent and Carmen again. They give an appropriate aura of decadence to the place and hint at the sexual games Carmen is playing with Eddie. Carmen is the most underdeveloped character but she is obviously directing Vincent's actions. Mary Elizabeth Mastrantonio plays this role wonderfully, and whilst Vincent and Eddie interact, you can see Carmen's eyes making sure that Vincent is doing what she wants.

Moral: Eddie: "You gotta be a student of human moves."

Seeing: As with the fights in *Raging Bull*, every pool game is shot in a different style. In one game, Eddie enters to find Vincent the centre of attention as he plays a game and twirls the cue stick like a kung fu weapon. Vincent is in the centre of the frame throughout the whole sequence because he is performing and everybody is looking at him. As Vincent moves around the table, the camera moves around the table also, at a fixed distance. Although Scorsese often uses the camera to show externally what the central characters are feeling inside, we don't often get point of view shots. In one sequence, Eddie (the student of human moves, remember) scans a pool hall and we see what he scans. The camera suddenly stops and whips back to one of the players in the room, showing us that Eddie has spotted his prey.

Hearing: The soundtrack is heavy with blues, R&B, rock and classical music as the characters move between the different environments. Vincent's kung fu performance to Warren Zevon's 'Werewolves Of London' is a standout sequence.

Subtext: The 1980s were about money, and this film manages to hoodwink the audience into thinking it is about money because that's what all the talk is about. Just listen to a few of Eddie's lines: "I never kid about money"; "Money won is twice as sweet as money earned"; and "You smell what I can smell?" (i.e. money). So the film is about how Eddie Felson educates and corrupts sweet, naïve Vincent and not-so-sweet and naïve Carmen. This education continues right up to the mesmerising scene where Eddie starts playing again and allows himself to be suckered by Amos (a lovely piece of work by Forest Whitaker). Eddie keeps paying out to Amos, allowing himself to 'show his ass.' By making himself a sucker, Eddie is punishing himself, as all Scorsese heroes must do. This renewal process is also cleansing his soul of his past sins (Scorsese has a shot of Eddie emerging from water at a swimming pool), starting again as a pure being. Eddie gets back into physical and mental shape, so that by the time he sees Vincent and Carmen again, he sees what monsters he has created. (He even has new glasses, so that he can see clearly again.) Although the film ends on a Hollywood high note, Eddie knows that he has made a mistake and so must try to reform Vincent and Carmen.

This is one reading of the film, but it can also be read several ways because of the ambiguity of Eddie's motivations. Did he use Vincent and Carmen so that he could work up the courage to get back into the game? Are his motives purely selfish and he wants nothing more than to be the best in the world? Is everything he said before his 'cleansing' bullshit?

Background: Scorsese was approached to direct this by Paul Newman, who had a script, and Scorsese agreed to do it if the script could be rewritten by novelist/screen-writer Richard Price. Price is best known for his poetic/tough street dialogue, which later saw him deliver some sharp scripts for *Sea Of Love* (1989), *Night And The City* (1992), *Clockers* (1995), *Ransom* (1996) and *Shaft* (2000). So Newman, Scorsese and Price researched, rewrote and discussed the script so that it was tailored for

Newman. It was a star vehicle for him and both Scorsese and Price knew it. As usual Scorsese prepared detailed notes on every shot – every time he got an idea he put it on a Post-it note and would collect them from around his house every day. There were almost 400 set-ups for the 10-week shoot. Newman and Cruise did all their own cue work, except for one of Cruise's trick shots, and they were surrounded by many of the top players as actors and advisors. All the hard work and planning worked out for the best. Disney made over $50 million out of their $10 million investment.

Verdict: For all the fantastic technical achievements, what we have here is a sports movie that adheres to the conventions of the genre. See *Karate Kid*, *Rocky* et al. for other examples of this very Hollywood genre. 3/5

Armani Commercial 1 (1986)

Cast: Christophe Bouquin, Christina Marsilach

Crew: Director/Treatment: Martin Scorsese, Producer: Barbara De Fina, Cinematographer: Néstor Almendros, B&W, 30 seconds

Story: On a bed, a woman teaches a man some Italian words by touching her body and saying the words.

Background: Scorsese said that he originally had the couple naked, until he realised it was an advert for clothes.

Bad (1987)

Cast: Michael Jackson (Darryl), Alberto Alejandrino (Hispanic Man), Paul Calderon (Dealer), Horace Daily (Street Bum), Roberta Flack (Darryl's Mother), Marvin Foster (Crack Customer), Greg Holtz Jr. (Cowboy), Adam Nathan (Tip), Jaime Perry (Ski), Pedro Sanchez (Nelson), Wesley Snipes (Mini Max)

Crew: Director: Martin Scorsese, Writer: Richard Price, Producers: Barbara De Fina, Quincy Jones, Cinematographer: Michael Chapman, Editor: Thelma Schoonmaker, Composer: Michael Jackson, Choreographers: Gregg Burge, Jeffrey Daniel, Michael Jackson, B & W/Colour, 16 mins

Story: College boy Darryl travels home via the train. Somebody on the train asks him, "How many guys proud of you?" "Three," he says. When he gets home, his mother is at work so he has to look after himself. Hanging out with his three friends, it becomes obvious that Darryl is different to his friends – the tension is created between his education and their lack of it. Mini Max asks if Darryl is bad. Darryl decides to prove it by mugging an old man in the subway. As the mugging is going down, Darryl changes his mind and tells his friends that they shouldn't do it. (Cue song.) Darryl and his friends part.

Cine-Literate: Black and white spirit of *The Cool World* (dir Shirley Clarke, 1963). Gang choreography of *West Side Story* (dirs Robert Wise, Jerome Robbins, 1961). Colour and movement of Vincente Minnelli musicals.

Home Movie: Catherine and Charlie are passengers on the subway. Marty is the wanted man on the poster.

Voice-Over: The letter from Darryl's mother is read by Roberta Flack's voice-over.

Seeing: This is shot in grainy black and white, the song is in colour – very *The Wizard Of Oz*. There is a long pan around Darryl's apartment. The camera twists around Jackson's body at a fixed distance. One sequence is similar to the *Mean Streets* party scene, where the camera is a fixed distance from Jackson's face as he moves. There is a lot of reverse tracking during the dancing and symmetrical framing. Scorsese uses the gridlike subway to move the camera in rigid forward/backward, left/right directions.

Hearing: It's a music video! The hissing steam of the subway and the whooshes as people whiplash arms, heads, feet around to the dance are perfectly synchronised to the music, giving point/counterpoint. The 'breakdown' at the end of the song, where Jackson chants without music and is echoed by the dancers, was shot in one take with three cameras.

Subtext: Darryl's nice world of college contrasts with the corrupt, drug dealing and mugging world of Harlem. Darryl is trapped by his past and his associations. He has to stand up to them. The implication is that in the past Darryl was violent, that he lived a double life of education and crime. In this film he decides to leave his old society for his new one.

Background: Immediately after finishing *The Color Of Money*, Scorsese received an unexpected commission from Michael Jackson. He was happy to spend $2 million so that he could move the camera around and emulate the musicals of Vincente Minnelli, as he had done on *New York, New York* and *The Last Waltz*.

Verdict: It is a simple, sombre tale, where the still, black and white story starkly contrasts with the moving, colour song. The song represents Darryl's emotions/thoughts/dreams, which are more alive than his life. It's good, not bad. 3/5

Somewhere Down The Crazy River (1988)

Cast: Robbie Robertson, Sammy BoDean, Maria McKee

Crew: Director/Treatment: Martin Scorsese, Producers: Amanda Pirie, Tim Clawson, Cinematographer: Mark Plummer, Colour, 4.5 mins

Story: This music video has Robbie singing to the camera and then embracing a woman.

The Last Temptation Of Christ (1988)

Cast: Willem Dafoe (Jesus), Harvey Keitel (Juda), Barbara Hershey (Mary Magdalene), Verna Bloom (Mary, Mother of Jesus), Gary Basaraba (Andrew, Apostle), Irvin Kershner (Zebedee), Victor Argo (Peter, Apostle), Michael Been (John, Apostle), Paul Herman (Phillip, Apostle), John Lurie (James, Apostle), Leo Burmester (Nathaniel, Apostle), Andre Gregory (John the Baptist), Alan Rosenberg (Thomas, Apostle), Harry Dean Stanton (Saul/Paul), David Bowie (Pontius Pilate), Leo Marks (Voice of Temptation/Satan)

Crew: Director: Martin Scorsese, Writer: Paul Schrader, Novel: Nikos Kazantzakis, Producers: Barbara De Fina, Harry J Ufland (Executive), Cinematographer: Michael Ballhaus, Editor: Thelma Schoonmaker, Composers: Peter Gabriel, Shankar (Additional Music), 164 mins

Story: Jesus is a carpenter who makes crosses for Roman crucifixions. This is a way of making himself a sinner. He receives God as a shrieking bird of prey digging its claws into his head, so he sins to keep God away from him and to prevent himself from becoming God's pawn. Previously he had rejected Mary Magdalene's love and she became a prostitute (she has the sweat of nations on her skin), so he asks her forgiveness as he goes into the desert to try to find out what God wants from him. His first faltering steps give him a small following. He tells his friend Juda that he is a rebel but that he is afraid of the path he must take. Juda is a man of action, a zealot who has been ordered to kill Jesus, but he tells Jesus that he will let him live for as long as he stays on the right path. John the Baptist sends Jesus into the desert, where he is tempted by Satan, and upon his return he declares war on evil. Jesus decides to lead a crowd to the Jewish temple in Jerusalem with the intention of destroying it, but he fails to lift a hand against it and is eventually betrayed to the Romans by his friend Juda. Roman Pontius Pilate tells Jesus that he is dangerous because he wants to change the way people think. Jesus is crucified but moments before his death an angel saves him, saying that God had spared him. Jesus lives a normal life with women and children of his own, impervious to the suffering of the world. He is happy at last. On his deathbed, Juda and some of the other Apostles visit him, tell him he has been tricked by Satan and castigate Jesus for his lies. Realising his mistake, and fully aware of what he is giving up, Jesus begs forgiveness of God, is returned to the cross, and dies there saying "It is accomplished."

Wiseguy: Juda and Saul/Paul are zealots who are willing and able to kill. We see Juda kill a Roman soldier and Saul kill Lazarus.

Cine-Literate: The main problem with a spiritual film is how to portray the spiritual. In this case, Scorsese opted for the simple physicality of Pier Paolo Pasolini's *The Gospel According To St Matthew* (1964), which portrayed Jesus as a political animal wanting to rebel against the system. Scorsese has said that at the beginning of the film he wanted Jesus to be portrayed like the restless James Dean at the beginning of *Rebel Without A Cause* (Nicholas Ray, 1955). This physicality and tension is maintained throughout the film. For the scene when Jesus is nailed to the cross, Scorsese used the same shots as he had done for 'Big' Bill Shelly's crucifixion in *Boxcar Bertha*. Oh, and Leo Marks, the voice of Satan, is the screenwriter of *Peeping Tom* (Michael Powell, 1960).

Picture: There are pictures of lovemaking on Mary Magdalene's wall.

Voice-Over: Throughout the film we hear Jesus' thoughts as a loud whisper.

Moral: Jesus: "I'm a heart, so I love."

Seeing: The miracles have a natural quality to them. When the snakes, lion, fire and tree appear in front of Jesus in the desert, they are really there. When Jesus takes out his heart and offers it to his apostles, it does not evoke the wrenching body horror of David Cronenberg's *Videodrome* (1982), but conveys the intended message. It reminded me of Andrei Tarkovsky's films, where things just happen without announcement or reaction. By keeping the camera on the objects, the objects become mundane, and then become accepted as true.

Like Scorsese's 'street' movies, the camera swoops around people and at them. In one self-conscious but effective shot, Jesus is carrying his own cross with people around him, making a live-action rendition of Hieronymus Bosch's painting *The Ghent Christ Carrying The Cross* from the early 16th century.

Hearing: The impressive score by Peter Gabriel was performed by musicians from a variety of nationalities. In 1983, Scorsese gave Gabriel some ideas (including shepherd songs) to start him on the right track, and in the intervening years Gabriel researched sound archives and listened to authentic ethnic music. As a result the film moves seamlessly from Eastern music to African to Brazilian beats to English choirboy in a fusion of world music.

Subtext: The quote from Nikos Kazantzakis at the beginning of the film references his incessant battle between the spirit and the flesh, and this is a good description of what happens throughout the film, and perhaps could serve as the theme that links all of Scorsese's films. In some cases the comfort of the flesh wins (*The Age Of Innocence*, for example) whilst in *The Last Temptation Of Christ* the purity of the spirit wins. This difference (the Jekyll & Hyde), is best expressed when Jesus says that God is inside us and the Devil is in the world around us.

Rather than portray the spiritual as ethereal, Scorsese makes everything real and solid. So there is no floating. No auras. No 'spiritual' music or sound effects. Jesus is portrayed as a real man, who is afraid of what might happen to him. When he says to Juda, "I want to rebel but I'm afraid" he is referring to both his destiny (fear of God/spiritual), and to upsetting the world he lives in (fear of pain/physical).

Once Jesus has accepted his destiny, and that he is the Messiah, it is then a matter of how he translates God's news to the people. Juda and John the Baptist are very much Old Testament, believing one should respond with anger, whereas Jesus' way is to respond with love. So when Jesus holds up an axe and says he is going to war, Juda believes that Jesus will lead an army. However, as with his parables, the wielding of the axe is a physical symbol of what Jesus intends to do spiritually.

Background: After the abortive attempt to make the film with Paramount in 1983, Scorsese launched a leaner $7 million production that filmed on location in Morocco. This was a completely different filming experience for Scorsese. Without the bars and cars he usually had, Scorsese had to visualise with landscapes, uneven terrain, a dearth of roads and authentic buildings, not to mention the hot sun and a shooting schedule that was shortened by the sun setting around 4:30pm. With many set-ups needed, the cast did not have time to prepare and rehearse on set, so they got into character in make-up. Barbara Hershey remembered crying in preparation for the stoning sequence, and the make-up person being horrified, thinking she had done something wrong. Scorsese would talk to his actors between set-ups, while first assistant Joe Reidy and cinematographer Michael Ballhaus arranged extras and the camera (following Scorsese's sketches of course). It was physically demanding carrying equipment to such a remote location and so improvisation was the key, especially since a crane that was shipped from the United States never arrived. The last shot, where Jesus says "It is accomplished" is followed by a white out. This was not planned and was due to light leaking onto the film. Scorsese decided to use it. Plagued by controversy upon its release,

The Last Temptation Of Christ made back its budget with a little bit of change.

Verdict: There are things to complain about, like the American accents and the sometimes disjointed narrative early on, but overall it is a film that makes you think rather than feel. When it strays from the standard Gospel texts, it is for an intelligent and human reason, usually to show Jesus as a human figure rather than as an icon. As a result, his human fears and desires make him vulnerable to temptation. It is then all the more understandable that he would succumb to the last temptation, a human life with women and children. 3/5

Armani Commercial 2 (1986)

Cast: Jens Peter, Elisabetha Ranella

Crew: Director/Treatment: Martin Scorsese, Producer: Barbara De Fina, Cinematographer: Michael Ballhaus, Colour, 20 seconds

Story: A man watches a woman, while she watches him. He leaves, knocking over a bottle of perfume. She finds the perfume and smells it.

'Life Lessons' in New York Stories (1989)

Cast: Nick Nolte (Lionel Dobie), Rosanna Arquette (Paulette), Steve Buscemi (Gregory Stark), Patrick O'Neal (Phillip Fowler), Jesse Borrego (Reuben Toro), Illeana Douglas (Paulette's Friend), Debbie Harry (Girl at Blind Alley), Peter Gabriel (Himself), Victor Argo (Cop), Richard Price (Artist at Opening)

Crew: Director: Martin Scorsese, Writer: Richard Price, Producer: Barbara De Fina, Cinematographer: Néstor Almendros, Editor: Thelma Schoonmaker, 44 mins

Story: Lionel Dobie is a famous artist with three weeks to go until his next big show, but he is blocked. Paulette, his assistant/girlfriend, is also his muse and he needs her around to trigger his creativity, but she is off with a new boyfriend. They agree that she will stay if she doesn't have to sleep with Lionel. She fuels his libido, but he has no outlet for it other than the large canvas he is painting. The pair to and fro until Paulette leaves. At his show, Lionel looks at his painting, and then makes contact with another young artist. Looking at her lips/neck/hands ignites a new love/muse and he asks her to become his assistant.

Cine-Literate: Although Scorsese had worked with cinematographer Néstor Almendros on an Armani commercial in 1986, this was their first fiction film. Almendros had worked with Truffaut on many films and was known for his use of colour and his rapid speed between set-ups. Truffaut liked using an iris to concentrate the attention on a particular part of the screen, and Scorsese uses it here several times, including the very first and last shots.

Home Movie: Martin Scorsese (and his dog Zoe) have their photo taken with Lionel Dobie at the opening. The next photo is Dobie with director Michael Powell. Blink and you'll miss them.

Picture: The whole film is about the creation of a picture. This is the beast that drains Lionel of everything, yet gives him just enough nourishment to keep going. Paulette is the inspiration that gives the picture form.

Moral: Lionel Dobie: "It's art. You give it up, you were never an artist in the first place. You make art because you have to."

Seeing: In his SoHo loft, Lionel is alive and does all his thinking. Whilst in there, the world is full of music (Procul Harlem, The Rolling Stones, Bob Dylan) and what he sees/feels. These are represented with quick cutting and multiple points of view. We are looking at him create, and he is looking at what he is creating. We don't really see the painting until his big show.

Outside the loft, the world is quite normal and sedate, with Scorsese using relatively normal shooting and editing techniques. By making this contrast in his filming style, the loft becomes a magic place that we do not want to leave, echoing Lionel's obsession with and addiction to painting.

Hearing: We hear only what Lionel wants to hear, which is loud music and the scrape of paint across the canvas.

Subtext: In Truffaut's film about film-making, *Day for Night* (1973), director Ferrand's assistant Jöelle (Nathalie Baye) says that she "would leave a boyfriend for a film, but would not leave a film for a boyfriend." This idea that art is more important than life is Lionel's point of view. Whether or not that is also true for Scorsese is open to conjecture, but certainly he seems to portray this point of view with understanding.

Background: Woody Allen came up with the idea of making a compilation film of short stories, much like the Italian and French masters did in the 1950s and 1960s. Using New York as the setting, Woody Allen did a funny one (See my Pocket Essential on Woody Allen, written as Martin Fitzgerald), Francis Ford Coppola did a romantic one, and Scorsese did the dramatic one.

Scorsese had always wanted to do a version of Fyodor Dostoyevsky's *The Gambler* because of the central relationship of an older writer who is emotionally and artistically dependent upon a younger woman. In the novella, the young woman asks the writer to prove his love by insulting a noblewoman. (This idea becomes Lionel proving his love by kissing a cop.) The story is quite dark, but Scorsese added elements from the real-life relationship between Dostoyevsky and Polina Suslova to lighten the tone.

Verdict: An engaging look at artistic personalities. As with

New York, New York the artists are unequal in celebrity and development, which leads to friction and conflict. 3/5

Made In Milan (1990)

Cast: Giorgio Armani

Crew: Director: Martin Scorsese, Writer: Jay Cocks, Producer: Barbara De Fina, Cinematographer: Néstor Almendros, Editor: Thelma Schoonmaker, Composer: Howard Shore, 20 mins

Story: A short documentary about fashion designer Giorgio Armani, who talks about his fashion, his family history and the city of Milan.

GoodFellas (1990)

Cast: Robert De Niro (James "Jimmy" Conway), Ray Liotta (Henry Hill), Joe Pesci (Tommy DeVito), Lorraine Bracco (Karen Hill), Paul Sorvino (Paul "Paulie" Cicero), Frank Sivero (Frankie Carbone), Tony Darrow (Sonny Bunz), Mike Starr (Frenchy), Frank Vincent (Billy Batts), Henny Youngman (Himself), Margo Winkler (Belle Kessler), Jerry Vale (Himself), Christopher Serrone (Young Henry Hill), Robbie Vinton (Bobby Vinton), Illeana Douglas (Rosie), Samuel L Jackson (Stacks Edwards), Edward McDonald (Himself)

Crew: Director: Martin Scorsese, Writers: Nicholas Pileggi, Martin Scorsese, Book: *Wiseguy* Nicholas Pileggi,

Producers: Irwin Winkler, Barbara De Fina (Executive), Bruce S Pustin (Associate), Cinematographer: Michael Ballhaus, Editors: Thelma Schoonmaker, James Y Kwei, 146 mins

Story: Irish boy Henry Hill grows up in an Italian neighbourhood and runs all sorts of errands for the local gangsters. He grows up loving the life, making money the easy way and enjoying the benefits (suits, cars, women, best seats in the clubs, respect from the neighbourhood). He works as a team with Irish hard man Jimmy Conway, and Italian firebrand Tommy DeVito. After Jimmy masterminds the $6 million Lufthansa heist, he keeps all the money and kills off the other people involved. Luckily, Henry was not in on it. Tommy kills made man Billy Batts ('made' means being one of the inner circle and untouchable) and when the bosses find out, Tommy is killed. After Henry spends time in jail he becomes involved with drug dealing and boss Paulie turns his back on Henry. After being busted by the Narcs, Henry decides to rat on his friends and go into the witness protection program. He doesn't like the life, because he can't get good food anymore.

Wiseguy: Well, they are all wiseguys and wisegals.

Cine-Literate: There are numerous references to other movies. The last shot is of Tommy wearing a hat shooting directly at the audience. This is a reference to Edwin S Porter's *The Great Train Robbery* (1903), acknowledged by many as the first Western and hence the first gangster movie, where the villain George Barnes shoots at the camera at the end of the film. There are also a couple of references to *The King Of Comedy*. Henny Youngman's line "Take my wife . . . please!" is used by Rupert Pukpin in his routine. And Henry's last line, "I'm an average nobody. I get to live the rest of my life like a schnook," echoes the sentiments of Rupert's line "Better to be king for a night than a schmuck for a lifetime."

Home Movie: Catherine has a couple of lovely cameos as Tommy DeVito's mother. She adlibbed the dinner scene where Henry, Jimmy and Tommy eat whilst made man Billy Batts is in the boot of Henry's car. Tommy borrows his mother's knife so that he can cut up Billy. Charles plays made man Vinnie, who puts too many onions in the prison food, and is present when Tommy is whacked.

Voice-Over: The film is primarily told from Henry's point of view and then we suddenly get Karen's thoughts when they get married.

Moral: Jimmy gives some friendly advice to Henry: "Never rat on your friends and always keep your mouth shut."

Seeing: I've mentioned some of the long tracking shots and specific edits in the introduction. Watching the film again, I was struck by the freedom in the editing. If Henry has a bit more to say then the film just stops on a freeze frame to let him finish, and then starts up again when he has caught up. Also, the angular movement of the camera and the rapid editing when Henry becomes a paranoid drug dealer are nice ways of showing the inside of Henry's mind.

Subtext: Francis Ford Coppola's *The Godfather* established the idea that the Mafia were a big family and that there were certain rules that must be followed. It was a classy but sombre affair that made crime attractive. Martin Scorsese's *GoodFellas* developed the idea by having Henry Hill as a boy who found the life attractive. The film begins with Henry's voice-over: "As far back as I can remember, I always wanted to be a gangster." Just as Scorsese and his generation found *Scarface*, *The Roaring Twenties* and countless gangster movies attractive, and would have liked to have lived those lives, there is a feeling that Scorsese is projecting some of his guilty desires into Henry. Furthermore, even though it is a horrible story of murder and betrayal, at the end of the film Henry still yearns for his life as a gangster because he had lots of fun. They are always laughing at the black humour, at their mistakes, always supporting each other, always eating and drinking together.

This is not an operatic story about the machinations and tragedies of Mafia life but about the nuts and bolts of running the business. It's about unloading lorries full of cigarettes and liquor, and collecting protection money and trying to sell off silencers that a friend doesn't want to buy. The wiseguys just want to conduct business and make as much money as possible. As Henry Hill explains: "All they got from Paulie was protection from other guys looking to rip them off. That's what it's all about. That's what the FBI can never understand – that what Paulie and the organization offer is protection for the kinds of guys who can't go to the cops. They're like the police department for wiseguys." When something happens to disrupt the flow of money, like Tommy making too much noise and drawing attention to them, then the gangsters start killing to protect the business. The violence is matter of fact. "Everybody expects to take a beating sometime." And so are the killings. "Shooting people was a normal thing. It was no big deal." The documentary approach gives an insider's view of the world without it losing its mystique.

The people in this world work hard and play hard. They work for themselves, and so they work all the hours there are. They don't make enough money to retire, so they must continue finding creative ways to get money. They have families and family is very important to them, so we have the dichotomy where a man is prepared to be violent for his job, and then caring towards his family. This is a Jekyll & Hyde situation. The paradox of the wiseguys is that they would often help their own people in the community, and then rob them. So the community got mixed messages about them.

The impact of this film is such that it is now the overriding impression that people have of gangsters. The TV show *The Sopranos* uses the ambience of *GoodFellas* (Martin Scorsese had a cameo in the first series) and it has been reported that the wiseguys now copy the words and mannerisms of their fictional counterparts.

Background: Nicholas Pileggi's book *Wiseguy* had all the basic research and Scorsese added the visual interpretation of those events. The script went through twelve drafts to clarify the life of the wiseguys. The people also took on a life of their own when the actors read and played the parts. The relationship between Henry and Tommy came in part from the natural repartee that developed between Ray Liotta and Joe Pesci. In addition Pesci has a short temper and he allowed this to inform his performance. The famous scene where Tommy and Henry are joking around, and then Tommy becomes serious, was written and improvised by Pesci. The changes in the script were such that the original names were replaced. Tommy DeSimone became Tommy DeVito. Paul Vario became Paulie Cicero and Jimmy Burke became Jimmy Conway. Some real people were involved in the film. For example, U.S. Attorney Edward McDonald plays himself when he tries to persuade Henry and Karen Hill to enter the Witness Protection Program. One of Henry's real daughters plays one of the Maries in the wedding scene. The film grossed $47 million in America alone and was both a critical and commercial hit.

Verdict: This is the definitive exploration of the gangster lifestyle. Horrible but captivating. 5/5

4 King Of The Kinematograph

All films are a combination of elements. In Scorsese's films they are primarily a combination of image, voice-over, dialogue, music and the editing/timing between them. What is remarkable about his work from *GoodFellas* onwards is the way each of these elements play in point/counterpoint to each other throughout the film. It is like watching a virtuoso musician at the top of his form. To a certain extent, it doesn't really matter what he is playing, as long as you have the pleasure of experiencing it for yourself. This has made him king of the kinematograph.

Cape Fear (1991)

Cast: Robert De Niro (Max Cady), Nick Nolte (Sam J Bowden), Jessica Lange (Leigh Bowden), Juliette Lewis (Danielle Bowden), Joe Don Baker (Claude Kersek, Private Investigator), Robert Mitchum (Lieutenant Elgart), Gregory Peck (Lee Heller, Cady's Attorney), Martin Balsam (Judge), Illeana Douglas (Lori Davis), Fred Dalton Thompson (Tom Broadbent)

Crew: Director: Martin Scorsese, Writers: Wesley Strick, James R Webb (Earlier Screenplay), Book: *The Executioners*

John D MacDonald, Producers: Barbara De Fina, Robert De Niro, Kathleen Kennedy (Executive), Frank Marshall (Executive), Cinematographer: Freddie Francis, Editor: Thelma Schoonmaker, Composers: Elmer Bernstein (Adaptation & Arrangement), Bernard Herrmann (music from *Cape Fear* (1962)), 123 mins

Story: Max Cady is an unstoppable force of nature (maybe even of God) who is released from prison after 14 years and has only one purpose in mind: to make his lawyer Sam Bowden suffer for withholding evidence that may have prevented Max from going to jail. Max was a God-fearing illiterate when he went in, but he learned how to read, got himself an education and became a jail-house lawyer. Now Max harasses the Cady family using the law and staying just the right side of it, probing their weaknesses so that they will break apart. First he picks up court clerk Lori Davis and assaults her because she has a crush on Sam. She won't prosecute, and Sam's wife Leigh thinks that Sam and Lori are having an affair. The coals of old arguments are raked over and ignited. Max then moves in on Sam's 15-year-old daughter Danny, and seduces her over to his side in an intense scene. Sam resorts to getting three men to beat up Max, but Max survives to put a restraining order on Sam and serve a motion to get Sam disbarred. Bowden uses his family as bait. Max enters the Bowden house and kills both the maid and a private eye. The Bowdens flee to their houseboat on Cape Fear where the final showdown occurs. Max puts the family through Hell, but they survive.

Wiseguy: Max is not nice.

Cine-Literate: This film is heavily influenced by Alfred Hitchcock. It is a remake of the excellent 1962 thriller directed by J Lee Thompson that featured the work of Hitchcock regulars Production Designer Robert Boyle, Editor George Tomasini and Composer Bernard Herrmann. For the remake Scorsese brought in legendary Title Designer Saul Bass and Production Designer Henry Bumstead, who had both worked with Hitchcock. There are sequences that recall Hitchcock's *Vertigo*, most memorably the dreamlike sequence after Sam and Leigh make love, where Leigh gets up afterwards and puts on make-up in front of the mirror, still aroused but unsatisfied. The use of multiple colours over extreme close-ups of the face is a carry-over from *Vertigo*. The colours are 'explained' by the fireworks outside the house. Hitchcock also used fireworks as a substitute for sex in *To Catch A Thief*. The primary influence is the original film, and Scorsese acknowledges this by reusing Bernard Herrmann's original score, adapted and arranged by Elmer Bernstein. (Bernstein also used some of Herrmann's unused score for Hitchcock's *Torn Curtain*.) There are cameos for Robert Mitchum (as a cop), Gregory Peck (as a hypocritical lawyer) and Martin Balsam (as a judge). Robert De Niro's Hellfire and Damnation portrayal of Max Cady almost seems like a synthesis of Robert Mitchum's roles as both Max Cady in the original *Cape Fear* and the Preacher in *The Night Of The Hunter* (1955). (Oh, and for good measure, the title sequence uses outtakes from the title sequence that Saul Bass shot for *Seconds*.)

Home Movie: Catherine and Charles Scorsese play Fruit Stand Customers, while Domenica Scorsese is Danny's Girlfriend.

Picture: At the beginning of the film we see Max Cady's cell plastered with photos of powerful people, like Stalin and superheroes. Max sees himself as on a par with these figures. In fact, the shirt he wears when he picks up Lori is very reminiscent of the web design on Spiderman's costume.

Voice-Over: There is no voice-over but Danny introduces and closes the film with something like a school report, saying what a magical summer she had. It is clear that this is Max's legacy – he has influenced (polluted? violated?) Danny in a way that will remain with her forever. This is explicit in the school theatre scene, where Max has engineered a meeting alone with Danny, pretending that he is her new drama teacher. As Max gains her confidence, and she agrees that she had thought about him the night before (probably sexually), he asks to put his arm around her. He puts his hand to her cheek, caresses it and then puts his thumb in her mouth and she sucks it. This is dynamite. The audience holds their breath because the whole film revolves around Max's unspoken agenda that he will rape Danny and here he is making her a willing victim. You can easily see how he could entice young girls into his bed (which was the original charge he was arrested for) and in this respect he is reminiscent of Matthew/Sport in *Taxi Driver*. (The scene was largely improvised by the cast. De Niro put his thumb into Lori's mouth without telling her that he was going to do it, so the surprise on her face was genuine and she went with it. The first take was used because it was the most genuine.)

Moral: Max Cady to Sam Bowden: "You could say I'm here to save you." Although there is irony and double meanings to everything Max says, Max does save the family. By trying to break the family and to see how much they will go through to stay together, Max actually creates a stronger family unit at the end. Leigh says at one point: "I'd like to know just how strong we are, or how weak."

Seeing: For each film, Scorsese draws upon different visual styles and devices to take the film a step further than he has been before. What is noticeable here is the way he fills the screen with a blanket colour, or with extreme close-ups of parts of the body over a blanket colour, or the negative of that image. By switching between these devices in certain scenes, Scorsese creates a disorientating effect in the audience. If you stare at something and then close your eyes, a latent image is created on your retina, so that you can still see it. These images create the same effect of seeing something that is not there, which is a visual interpretation of the Cady figure. The Bowdens see Cady, even when he is not there.

Hitchcock also played with blocks of colours, and extreme close-ups of the face in *Vertigo*, most notably in the dream sequence halfway through the film when Scotty (James Stewart) breaks down and is in a mental institution. Hitchcock plays with colours in the film, mostly reds and greens, whereas Scorsese dresses Max in pure whites, and reds, while Sam remains resolutely grey.

Max Cady is an unstoppable and constant force. Scorsese shows this repeatedly. For example, when Cady leaves prison at the beginning he walks towards the camera and does not stop, even when he fills the frame. When he confronts people, he stays still and relaxed, continuing to talk and be in their presence until it becomes uncomfortable. Then when they try to talk back to him, he has already gone. This creates a feeling of agitation and frustration.

Subtext: The film uses the thriller format to explore the moral complexities of the public defender. 14 years earlier, Sam Bowden thought that Max Cady deserved to go to jail for rape and aggravated assault, so he buried a report on the woman that said she was promiscuous. This may have swayed the jury to give Max an acquittal. Max, quite rightly, thinks that this is wrong and harasses the Bowdens to get his revenge for losing 14 years of his life, for being raped in jail, and for losing contact with his own family. Max tells Sam: "You will learn about loss." A systematic chain of events ensue that teach the Bowdens about loss. It starts with the loss of their dog, and then they begin tearing each other apart.

This is *Old Testament* retribution, and Max's religious conviction is emphasised throughout the film. Not only does he have religious quotations and images tattooed all over his body, but Max quotes from *The Bible* at the drop of a hat. He tells Danny that "Every man carries a circle of Hell around his head like a halo." He directs Sam to the Book of Job, which is about how God tested Job by taking everything away from him. During the climatic scenes, Max tells Sam that he will be directed to the 9th circle of Hell, the circle of traitors, and in the scene where Leigh and Danny are the jury and God is the judge, Max pronounces Sam guilty of betraying his fellow man and of unjustly judging Max. He is lethal because his body and spirit are combined with one purpose: he is morally outraged at what has been done to him.

Background: The film was originally written by Wesley Strick with Steven Spielberg in mind. Spielberg was involved with the project (as was Robert De Niro) but he eventually passed and De Niro proposed it to Scorsese. Once Scorsese latched onto the idea of Cady breaking up a dysfunctional family, the film began to make sense to him and he accepted the project. There were other reasons as well: he owed Universal another film after they supported *The Last Temptation Of Christ*, and he wanted to do an all-out genre movie. Interestingly, it cost $35 million and grossed $79 million in the United States alone, making it his most successful film up to that date.

Verdict: This is a 'fun' movie and a great roller-coaster ride. 3/5

The Age Of Innocence (1993)

Cast: Daniel Day-Lewis (Newland Archer), Michelle Pfeiffer (Ellen Olenska), Winona Ryder (May Welland), Richard E Grant (Larry Lefferts), Alec McCowen (Sillerton Jackson), Geraldine Chaplin (Mrs Welland), Mary Beth Hurt (Regina Beaufort), Stuart Wilson (Julius Beaufort), Miriam Margolyes (Mrs Mingott), Siân Phillips (Mrs Archer), Carolyn Farina (Janey Archer), Michael Gough (Henry Van Der Luyden), Alexis Smith (Louisa Van Der Luyden), Norman Lloyd (Mr Letterblair), Jonathan Pryce (Monsieur Rivière), Joanne Woodward (Narrator), Claire Bloom (uncredited)

Crew: Director: Martin Scorsese, Writers: Jay Cocks, Martin Scorsese, Novel: Edith Wharton, Producers: Barbara De Fina, Bruce S Pustin, Joseph P Reidy (Associate), Cinematographer: Michael Ballhaus, Editor: Thelma Schoonmaker, Composer: Elmer Bernstein, 139 mins (US), 133 mins (UK)

Story: In New York circa 1870, Newland Archer is announcing his engagement to May Welland at the annual Beaufort's ball, when he meets childhood friend Countess Ellen Olenska. Ellen has just returned from Europe, where she made a bad marriage, and there is talk of her loose ways. As a result she is eradicated from society until the intervention of Newland Archer ensures she is embraced by society again. As Ellen's lawyer, Newland then advises her not to pursue a divorce because her husband would say things that would irrevocably damage Ellen's position within society. In the meantime, Newland and Ellen have fallen in love. They decide that they should not pursue their romance and that Newland should marry May. The marriage is made but Newland still desires Ellen (now without income) and they agree to consummate their relationship. Newland is on the brink of throwing up his marriage and his position within society. However, May and society arrange everything so that Countess Olenska is provided for in Europe, and Newland remains trapped in New York. Newland raises a family with May.

Cine-Literate: Scorsese has stated that the films that had the most influence on this one are: *Letter From An Unknown Woman* (Max Ophuls, 1948), *The Red Shoes* (1948), *The Heiress* (William Wyler, 1949) and *The Leopard* (Luchino Visconti, 1963). They all deal with repression and frustration within a society, and the struggle for love to escape the boundaries of society.

Home Movie: Martin Scorsese has a cameo as the photographer taking May's wedding picture, and Domenica Scorsese has a small role as Katie Blenker. The film is dedicated to Luciano Charles Scorsese.

Picture: New York society plasters its walls full of paintings, and these are used as indicators of the character of the society. Mostly these are civilised paintings of animals, or elegant people. Julius Beaufort displays a controversial nude. Occasionally, specific paintings are highlighted by Scorsese's camera, like the graphic depiction of Jenny McCrae being murdered by two Indians in 1777. This picture has several meanings. Firstly, the murder was the rallying call for the Patriot militia and so in a way was the beginning of American civilisation. It is appropriate that the painting is displayed at Mrs Mingott's house, since she is the matriarch of New York society and its link to the past. However, it also shows the contrast between the physical murders of the past and the spiritual murders of the present. We mustn't forget how violent current civilisation is, no matter what the veneer. When we see the paintings in Countess Olenska's rooms, they are free-form and loose, informal, in contrast to the precise, formal pictures elsewhere. When Newland looks into the face of a woman in a picture, she has no face – she is unknown, independent and free.

Voice-Over: The film is narrated by Joanne Woodward, presumably as the author Edith Wharton, who gives a Godlike view of the people and proceedings.

Moral: Newland Archer to Countess Ellen Olenska: "Everything is labelled, but everybody is not." Newland warns Ellen that people's intentions are different to their appearance, but it is HIS underestimation of people that leads to his imprisonment within society.

Seeing: The camera movements are impeccably and precisely composed, as always (has Scorsese never used a handheld camera?) but Scorsese tries something new with the editing. To make the film into one continuous, uninterrupted dance, he often uses dissolves rather than cuts in this film. There is a beautiful series of dissolves showing the Beaufort's ballroom covered in dust sheets, then with light coming in, then dressed up, then with people dancing. For some reason this sequence, plus the long crane shot following Newland through the drawing rooms to the ballroom, reminded me of the ball in Orson Welles' *The Magnificent Ambersons*. The dissolve also allowed Scorsese to cut out all the slow crane shots and just show the images he wanted from the sequence.

Sometimes the dissolves would be to colours that indicate something about the character or place. When Ellen gets yellow roses from Newland, it dissolves to yellow, for example. Flowers were used in the title sequence. Elaine and Saul Bass designed flowers blooming quickly behind curtains of lace. These blooms in gilded cages act as a precursor to the delicate emotions that are about to be trapped by society. The flowers, like the paintings, are subtle ways for these people to express themselves, but are also indicators that allow other people in the society to make judgements upon them. When Newland tells May that he sent flowers to Ellen, May tells Newland that other people also sent flowers to her but that Ellen never mentioned Newland's to her. Upon first viewing you infer that Newland is hurt by this slight on Ellen's part, or that Ellen wanted to keep the flowers a secret. Upon second viewing, knowing that May is in fact a master manipulator and therefore untrustworthy, we can see that May is putting the knife into Newland and twisting it to make him suffer.

Subtext: The film is about the rituals and surface of New York polite society which hide the true feelings and motivations of the society. The society has very precise rules and these are enforced with smiles. (I'm reminded of the line in *GoodFellas* when Henry tells us that murderers come with smiles.) The object is for the good families to be seen as good families, and for people to remain within the family. Thus, although Newland is presented as our hero, and a man who will put things right, he is unaware that his marriage to May is effectively an arranged marriage between two of the great families of New York. The coup de grace is performed by May at the end of the film, which is the first time that Newland realises that he is a prisoner within a gilded cage. Just as he has been manoeuvring people to help Ellen back into society, May had been manoeuvring society to prevent Newland from leaving her. Newland had dismissed her as being a vacuum behind a mask, but in the end she is a master manipulator par excellence. She had prevented Newland and Ellen from consummating their relationship by telling Ellen of her pregnancy a full two weeks before she knew she was pregnant. To turn the knife, the first dinner of the newly married couple is a going-away party for Ellen.

Newland is introduced to us as a man who questions things in private but conforms in public. At this stage he has the illusion of freedom. When it seems that he and Ellen may become an item, the first thing he does is run to May to speed up their marriage date – he is reverting to type. After the marriage, he tells Ellen: "You gave me my first glimpse of a real life. Then you asked me to go on with the false one. No one can endure that." "I'm enduring it," Ellen replies. They are in this situation because it is Newland's nature to act as he does, and his nature prevents him from being free. In the end, when he is old and has the opportunity to meet Ellen in Paris after May has died, Newland does not see her. Why? Perhaps because he is satisfied that Ellen is still in this world, and that he knows this. Perhaps because he realises that the idea of her, the fetish of her, is all he needed to survive.

Verdict: The opera being performed at the beginning of the film is *Faust*, wherein Faust sells his soul to the devil for the love of wealth and position, which is very appropriate for this film. As with other Scorsese films, this deals with a corrupt society that has its own rules, and the central character is trapped in that society, despite his obsession with Countess Olenska. A fascinating and undervalued film, I think. 4/5

Casino (1995)

Cast: Robert De Niro (Sam "Ace" Rothstein), Sharon Stone (Ginger McKenna-Rothstein), Joe Pesci (Nicholas "Nicky" Santoro Sr.), James Woods (Lester Diamond), Don Rickles (Billy Sherbert), Alan King (Andy Stone), Kevin Pollak (Phillip Green), L Q Jones (Commissioner Pat Webb), Dick Smothers (Senator), Frank Vincent (Frank Marino), John Bloom (Don Ward), Pasquale Cajano (Boss Remo Gaggi), Melissa Prophet (Jennifer Santoro), Bill Allison (John Nance), Vinny Vella (Artie Piscano), Oscar Goodman (Himself), Frankie Avalon (Himself), Steve Allen (Himself), Jayne Meadows (Herself), Jerry Vale (Himself)

Crew: Director: Martin Scorsese, Writers: Nicholas Pileggi, Martin Scorsese, Book: Nicholas Pileggi, Producers: Barbara De Fina, Joseph P Reidy (Associate), Cinematographer: Robert Richardson, Editor: Thelma Schoonmaker, 178 mins (US),171 mins (UK)

Story: As with *GoodFellas*, this is an extended documentary on the working life of the Mafia, only this concentrates on their history in Las Vegas. Specifically, the Tangiers casino managed by Sam "Ace" Rothstein. We see how the skim works: the people bet money and lose; the money goes into the counting room; a man with a suitcase goes into the counting room, fills the suitcase and leaves without anybody seeing him; the money is delivered to the back room of an Italian grocery in Kansas and given to the Mafia bosses. The three main characters are placed in this milieu: Sam "Ace" Rothstein knows every gambling trick in the book, and so is the perfect manager for a Mob-run casino; Nicholas "Nicky" Santoro Sr. is the muscle who makes sure that Sam is protected from outside forces; Ginger McKenna is the prostitute and hustler that Ace falls for and marries. We follow Ace, a control freak, as his delusions of grandeur and self-importance lead to his own destruction. We follow Nicky as his strong-arm tactics result in him working outside the bosses' itinerary, and lead to him being killed. We follow Ginger as Ace's controlling influence stifles and suffocates her, leading her to alcohol, drugs and an eventual overdose. In the end, the bosses had the perfect scam, the perfect way of making money, but they lost it all because everybody up and down the line just got greedier and greedier.

Wiseguy: Yep, full of wiseguys and wisegals again.

Cine-Literate: Although there are allusions to other movies, like using Georges Delerue's music from Jean-Luc Godard's *Le Mépris* (1963), this feels like a Scorsese picture through and through.

Home Movie: Catherine Scorsese has another lovely cameo as Mrs Piscano, who flinches every time her husband swears. As well as being funny, this is a comment upon the people who criticised *GoodFellas* for all its swearing ("Fuck" is said 246 times). As it happens, "Fuck" is said 362 times in *Casino*. Catherine T Scorsese is Piscano's Daughter as well as Assistant Property Master behind the scenes.

Voice-Over: Sam's dry, factual narration is in complete contrast to Nicky's spicy, humorous narration. Nicky: "A lot of holes in the desert, and a lot of problems are buried in those holes. But you gotta do it right. I mean, you gotta have the hole already dug before you show up with a package in the trunk. Otherwise, you're talking about a half-hour to forty-five minutes worth of digging. And who knows who's gonna come along in that time? Pretty soon, you gotta dig a few more holes. You could be there all fuckin' night." Significantly, Ginger does not have a voice in the film, which emphasises both our uncertainty about her motivation and is in line with Ace's plan to keep her controlled.

Moral: Sam "Ace" Rothstein: "When you love someone,

you've gotta trust them. There's no other way. You've got to give them the key to everything that's yours. Otherwise, what's the point? And, for a while, I believed that's the kind of love I had." Like the Mafia, Ace says he relies on trust, and then he keeps tabs on Ginger because he doesn't trust her. This paranoia is directly analogous to the Mafia's definition of 'trust.'

Subtext: Nicky is the true character. He is the one who sees everything as it truly is. Whereas Ace gets sucked into the dream and glamour of Vegas, the country clubs, the flashy apartments and houses and the cars, and the trophy wife that everybody can admire, Nicky stays true to his roots and opens a restaurant, keeping it small and realistic. Ace Rothstein knows and fears Nicky's directness: "No matter how big a guy was, Nicky would take him on. You beat Nicky with fists, he comes back with a bat; you beat him with a knife, he comes back with a gun; and if you beat him with a gun, you better kill 'em, 'cause he'll be coming back and back, until one of you is dead."

Ace is sucked into this new world because he thinks his sins have been absolved. He says at one stage: "Running a casino is like robbing a bank with no cops around. For guys like me, Las Vegas washes away your sins. It's like a morality car wash." And this religious theme is continued when he refers to the counting room as the "holy of holies", and calls the bosses "the Gods." This last remark is confirmed by an image of the bosses arranged as if it is the Last Supper lit by Franz Hals.

Background: Another film with Nicholas Pileggi, based

on real people and events. However, once the facts have been through Scorsese's filtering system, we end up with something that has the form needed for a film. So Frank "Lefty" Rosenthal becomes Sam "Ace" Rothstein and Anthony "Tony The Ant" Spilotro becomes Nicky Santoro and Geri McGee becomes Ginger McKenna. The Tangiers casino is fictional. In reality Rosenthal managed four casinos on the Strip: the Stardust, the Fremont, the Frontier and the Marina. Released on 22 November 1995, the film grossed over $42 million in the US alone against a budget of $52 million and Sharon Stone earned an Oscar nomination for her role.

Verdict: When Ace keeps a Japanese high roller from leaving the country, and gets him back on the gaming table, he reveals the policy of Las Vegas: "In the casino, the cardinal rule is to keep them playing and to keep them coming back. The longer they play, the more they lose, and in the end, we get it all." But even when they (Ace, Nicky, Ginger, the bosses) have it all, it is not enough, because it is in their nature to want more or something else. In *Casino*, Scorsese reveals the folly of human endeavour. 4/5

A Personal Journey with Martin Scorsese Through American Movies (1995)

Cast: Martin Scorsese (Narrator/Host), Francis Ford Coppola, Brian De Palma, Clint Eastwood, Fritz Lang, Gregory Peck, Arthur Penn, King Vidor, Billy Wilder

Crew: Directors & Writers: Martin Scorsese & Michael Henry Wilson, Producers: Florence Dauman, Martin Scorsese, Raffaele Donato (Associate), Bob Last (Executive), Colin MacCabe (Executive), Dale Ann Stieber (Line), Cinematographers: Jean-Yves Escoffier, Frances Reid, Nancy Schreiber, Editors: Kenneth Levis, David Lindblom, Composer: Elmer Bernstein, 225 mins

Story/Cine-Literate/Home Movie: Scorsese narrates a history of American film using the works of directors that interest him. His tastes are catholic, so we get clips from everybody from Edwin S Porter and DW Griffith to John Cassavetes and Samuel Fuller. It's separated into chapters: The Director's Dilemma deals with the director working within the Hollywood Studio system; The Director as Storyteller shows the genres (Western, Gangster, Musical) that directors used to create fiction rather than reveal reality; The Director as Illusionist shows the technical processes that directors have embraced to enhance their stories; The Director as Smuggler gives examples of directors who plant subtext in their films; and The Director as Iconoclast is for those directors who take on the system.

Moral: Frank Capra says it all, "One man, one film." The auteur theory in a nutshell.

Verdict: Scorsese has never been shy about his film influences, but this is interesting because by not including the Powell & Pressburger films, or the Italian neorealists, I suddenly realised that Scorsese is living a sort of schizophrenic existence as a film-maker. Is he making his films for money (*The Color of Money*, *Cape Fear*), or for himself (*Kundun*)? Is he smuggling messages (*The King of Comedy*) or taking on the system (*The Last Temptation of Christ*)? This leisurely walk through film history raises more questions about Scorsese than provides answers. 3/5

Kundun (1997)

Cast: Tenzin Thuthob Tsarong (Dalai Lama (Adult)), Gyurme Tethong (Dalai Lama (Aged 10)), Tulku Jamyang Kunga Tenzin (Dalai Lama (Aged 5)), Tenzin Yeshi Paichang (Dalai Lama (Aged 2)), Tencho Gyalpo (Dalai Lama's Mother), Tsewang Migyur Khangsar (Dalai Lama's Father), Geshi Yeshi Gyatso (Lama of Sera), Sonam Phuntsok (Reting Rimpoche), Lobsang Samten (Master of the Kitchen), Gyatso Lukhang (Lord Chamberlain), Jigme Tsarong (Taktra Rimpoche), Tenzin Trinley (Ling Rimpoche), Robert Lin (Chairman Mao)

Crew: Director: Martin Scorsese, Writer: Melissa Mathison, Producers: Barbara De Fina, Melissa Mathison, Cinematographer: Roger Deakins, Editor: Thelma Schoonmaker, Composer: Philip Glass, 128 mins

Story: The 14th Dalai Lama (called Kundun) is discovered reincarnated in a Tibetan province near the Chinese border. After a test where he picks out the objects owned by the 13th Dalai Lama, the young boy is brought to Lhasa and is educated. Although he lives a closeted existence, he is very modern and outward looking, wanting to know the world outside his window (using a telescope), and about the world outside Tibet (using a movie projector, a radio and books). When the Chinese invade Tibet and slaughter thousands of people, the Dalai Lama refuses to leave. Instead he goes to China and listens to what Chairman Mao has to say. The Dalai Lama practises his belief of non-violence and compassion, believing that the aggressors will become wise and stop fighting. When his life is threatened, he flees Tibet and finds sanctuary just across the border in India.

Wiseguy: Chairman Mao is presented as a hypocrite and bully.

Cine-Literate: When the Dalai Lama finds the gifts left by other countries, he watches films on a movie projector, including *La Poule aux oeufs d'or* (*The Goose that Laid the Golden Egg*, Georges Méliès, 1905), a newsreel of the Atom Bomb and *Henry V* (Laurence Olivier, 1945).

Home Movie: The film is dedicated to Catherine Scorsese (1912-1997).

Picture: The opening titles and the 'escape' sequence show a colourful sand painting of a mandala. (This is reminiscent of the painting that opens Jean Renoir's *The River* (1950).) The mandala is a representation of the universe that symbolises a striving for unity of self and completeness. The sand is eventually collected and poured into a lake, meaning that "all is nothing."

Moral: "You are here to love all living things." "All beings wish to find their purer selves."

Seeing: Rather than show the gore and suffering of the Tibetan people in a direct manner, Scorsese chooses to show the serenity and purity of the Dalai Lama. He is defiled by the violence – Scorsese represents this in an extraordinary image of blood invading the pure water of a pond (a shot repeated from *The Last Temptation Of Christ* when Jesus takes out his heart and offers it to his apostles).

The opening shot is of clouds at the peak of a mountain. It is only at the end, when the Dalai Lama is in India and he sets up his telescope, that we see that this mountain is all that he can see of Tibet once he has left. So the film, in a sense, becomes a remembrance. There is an echo of the mountain image when the sand painting is being swept up – in slow motion a cloud of sand particles go over a pile of sand.

The motif of seeing is continued throughout the film. As well as the film projector and the telescope (in one sequence the eye of the Dalai Lama is superimposed over the telescope lens), the monks also have visions. We don't always see these visions, but the monks trust their visions – they are just as real as things that they can touch. (Does Scorsese believe that his visions are just as real as things he can touch?) When we see the visions, like the massacre of thousands of Tibetans, they are real to us as well because we believe the visions we are seeing on the screen. The most interesting dream, though, is when the Dalai Lama dreams that the Chinese soldiers are talking to him, explaining that under Chairman Mao they are better off. This humanisation of Communism shows that perhaps there is a possibility that Tibet can change as well. Kundun acts on his dream and meets Chairman Mao, only to be told that "Religion is poison." From that moment, Kundun knows that Tibet is in real trouble, and that Mao plans to exterminate the monks.

As in other films, Scorsese uses Kurosawa's three dissolve close-up, but in this film he does something quite beautiful with the effect by doing a multiple dissolve close-up. It seems to be a film version of religious paintings where a figure is shown with multiple auras. Here, Scorsese gives the impression of multiple Kunduns as we get closer to him because of the 'ripple' effect of the dissolves.

Hearing: Mention must be made of Philip Glass' excellent score, which incorporates traditional instruments and sounds.

Subtext: Like *Mean Streets*, *Kundun* is a film about frustration. The Dalai Lama is unable to prevent his people from being overpowered and oppressed by China because of the non-violence he practises.

It would be very easy to compare *The Last Temptation Of Christ* and *Kundun* because of their religious subject matter, but that would be unfair because they have different intentions. As Gavin Smith points out in *Film Comment*: 'But where the Christ of *Last Temptation* trades in his low self-esteem for an exultant sense of revolutionary mission, the Buddha-child Dalai Lama of *Kundun* follows a reverse trajectory: from egocentric infant to selfless religious statesman.'

Kundun is almost a mirror image of Scorsese's usual narcissistic protagonists. When the border guard asks him if he is the Lord Buddha, Kundun replies: "I believe I am a reflection, like the moon on water. When you see me, and I try to be a good man, you see yourself." Kundun reflects the good parts of ourselves, whereas Scorsese's films usually have major protagonists that reflect the bad part of ourselves.

At the end of the film, Kundun has become the ocean of wisdom. He has grown up and become the spiritual leader of his country.

Background: Although Scorsese likes to nurture his own projects, this one was given to him by writer Melissa Mathison. After punching out 14 drafts, the film went into production using non-actors and was mostly shot in Morocco. As Scorsese pointed out: "Tibetan film, Catholic making it, written by a Buddhist, shot in a Moslem country, with the call to prayer every day." Unfortunately, this film failed to call many people to the cinema and it pulled a measly $5.5 million against a budget of $28 million. A great pity for such a great film.

Verdict: When I first saw this film, I thought it was beautiful but heavy. This 'heaviness' is quite common with Scorsese films because of the amount of information in them, and the 'alien' environments. With subsequent viewings, Scorsese's films become lighter. This film becomes radiant. 5/5

Il Dolce Cinema (1999)

Cast: Martin Scorsese (Host)

Crew: Director: Martin Scorsese, Writers: Suso Cecchi D'Amico, Martin Scorsese, Producers: Giorgio Armani, Barbara De Fina, Giuliana Del Punta, Bruno Restuccia, Cinematographer: Phil Abraham

Background: Like Martin Scorsese's history of American film, this is a similar examination of Italian film history (also known as *My Voyage To Italy*), using some of Scorsese's personal recollections and a hell of a lot of clips. It has everything from *Cabiria*, through to the Italian Neorealism of Roberto Rossellini and Vitorio De Sica, the aesthetics of Michelangelo Antonioni and the dreams of Federico Fellini, Pier Paulo Pasolini and Luchino Visconti. Quite a lot to cover, but at nearly four hours in length, Scorsese manages to do it.

Bringing Out the Dead (1999)

Cast: Nicolas Cage (Frank Pierce), Patricia Arquette (Mary Burke), John Goodman (Larry), Ving Rhames (Marcus), Tom Sizemore (Tom Walls), Marc Anthony (Noel), Mary Beth Hurt (Nurse Constance), Queen Latifah (Voice of Dispatcher Love)

Crew: Director: Martin Scorsese, Writer: Paul Schrader, Novel: Joe Connelly, Producers: Barbara De Fina, Scott Rudin, Joseph P Reidy, Eric Steel, Mark Roybal

(Associate), Jeff Levine (Associate), Bruce S Pustin (Executive), Adam Schroeder (Executive), Cinematographer: Robert Richardson, Editor: Thelma Schoonmaker, Composer: Elmer Bernstein, 120 mins

Story: Told over three nights, this is the story of paramedic Frank Pierce, who cares too much about the people he failed to bring back to life. "I hadn't saved anyone in months." Frank had been desensitised to the world, but then he failed to save a young street woman, Rose, and his guilt took over. Now he sees Rose in every person on the street and the guilt is killing him. As his episodic life unfurls, Frank becomes attached to Mary Burke and her dying father, whom he brought back to life. However, the comatose father speaks to Frank and in the end Frank decides to let the father die rather than prolong a useless existence. So Frank shows compassion, not by saving a life (it is Frank's narcissistic wish to save other people, regardless of the result), but by allowing it to end. (I'm reminded of a quote from *Kundun*: "Every result, whether good or bad, has a cost.")

Cine-Literate: Throughout the film, I kept thinking of two other films: Peter Yates' *Mother, Jugs And Speed* (1976), a black comedy about rival freelance ambulance companies; and especially *Catch-22* (Mike Nichols, 1970), a black comedy about the horror of war. The scene where drug dealer Curtis is impaled on an iron balustrade 52 floors up and in his dementia sees fireworks above the city is Scorsese's homage to Woody Allen's *Manhattan*.

Home Movie: Listen out for Martin Scorsese as the voice of one of the dispatchers. A nice performance.

Picture: The picture that Frank keeps in his head is of Rose's face. As he passes people on the street they take on the appearance of the woman he failed to save.

Voice-Over: Frank Pierce.

Moral: "You have to keep the body going until the brain and the heart recover enough to go on their own."

Seeing: The film is shot subjectively from Frank's point of view. It is the point of view of a stressed man, when the mind and body are at their lowest ebb, a perpetual four in the morning. So, from the eyes bathed in red at the beginning, to the speeded up ambulance and the hypersensitivity, everything is slightly weird.

The sequence where Frank remembers trying to save Rose has a weird feel to it because it was acted in reverse and the film was played backwards. There is also a surreal dream sequence where Frank walks along the street helping the dead rise from out of the ground.

Hearing: The soundtrack has music from the early 1990s and before.

Subtext: We live in a desensitised world. We block out all the horrible images that bombard us through newspapers and television. We walk the streets studiously wiping from vision and memory anything that might be distasteful and upset our status quo. We have an obligation to others, to feel compassion for them, and this film shows how Frank tries to regain the balance between his compassion and the guilt he feels. At one point Frank says in voice-over: "Saving someone's life is like falling in love. The best drug in the world. For days, sometimes weeks afterwards, you walk the streets, making infinite whatever you see. Once, for a few weeks, I couldn't feel the earth – everything I touched became lighter. Horns played in my shoes. Flowers fell from my pockets. You wonder if you've become immortal, as if you've saved your own life as well. God has passed through you. Why deny it, that for a moment there – God was you?" In the end Frank forgives himself for his narcissism, and realises that his job is to bear witness. "I realised that my training was useful in less than ten percent of the calls, and saving lives was rarer than that. After a while, I grew to understand that my role was less about saving lives than about bearing witness. I was a grief mop. It was enough that I simply turned up."

Background: Having directed a film about a passive character who feels compassion for living things, Scorsese directs a film about a passive character who feels compassion for the dead people he failed to save. The 75-night shoot was gruelling for Scorsese, but he was back on home turf again – in the Manhattan he knew. However, the finished film again failed to resonate with an audience. Budgeted at $32 million, it recouped half of that in America and struggled to find the rest around the world.

Verdict: Although I can admire the sincere sensibility

behind the film and the techniques used, the film does not take me out of myself like other Scorsese films. Watching *Taxi Driver*, I am in Travis Bickle's world. Similarly for *Raging Bull* and *GoodFellas* and *Casino*, I am in a place that Scorsese makes interesting for me. *Bringing Out The Dead* does not feel right. There is something missing. 2/5

Gangs Of New York (2002)

Cast: Leonardo DiCaprio (Amsterdam Vallon), Daniel Day-Lewis (William 'Bill the Butcher' Cutting), Cameron Diaz (Jenny Everdeane), Jim Broadbent (William 'Boss' Tweed), Henry Thomas (Johnny Sirocco), Liam Neeson (Priest Vallon, Amsterdam's Father), Brendan Gleeson (Walter 'Monk' McGinn), John C Reilly ('Happy' Jack Mulraney)

Crew: Director: Martin Scorsese, Writers: Jay Cocks, Kenneth Lonergan, Steven Zaillian, Book: Herbert Asbury, Producers: Alberto Grimaldi, Martin Scorsese, Laura Fattori (Line), Gerry Robert Byrne (Associate), Harvey Weinstein (Executive), Maurizio Grimaldi (Executive), Michael Hausman (Executive), Cinematographer: Michael Ballhaus, Editor: Thelma Schoonmaker, Composer: Howard Shore, 167 mins

Story: In 1946, during a fight between rival New York Gangs, Priest Vallon of the Dead Rabbits is killed by William Cutting (Bill the Butcher) of the Federation of American Natives. Vallon's son steals the knife that killed his father and ends up in a home for young offenders. Sixteen years later, Amsterdam Vallon leaves the home (they kept him in for longer because he tried to escape) and eventually becomes Bill's right hand man. He is confused by conflicting feelings: he wants revenge for his father's death but Bill is his new father-figure; he wants to bed Jenny Everdeane but she seems to be Bill's girl. After he beds Jenny, Amsterdam decides to kill Bill using the knife that killed his father. He fails, and is badly beaten and marked by Bill. Hiding out in the new church, Amsterdam finds religion and his Irish roots, restarts the Dead Rabbits and becomes a man of power to rival Bill. As all the gangs of New York begin their big face-off, they are overtaken and overpowered by the Draft Riots (citizens of New York refused to be drafted into the Union Army to fight in the Civil War whilst rich people were allowed to buy themselves out of the army, so the city rioted). Amsterda kills Bill. Modern America is forged out of this bloody mess.

Wiseguy: Billy boy.

Cine-Literate: The opening, bludgeoning fight sequence is cut like Orson Welles' *Chimes At Midnight/Falstaff* (1962), and the closing fight sequence is more akin to Akira Kurosawa's *Sanjuro* (1962).

Home Movie: Jenny changes her appearance and enters a rich household as a chambermaid. We see that she is in the house of Martin Scorsese, a rich man surrounded by his family.

Picture: Bill keeps a picture of Priest Vallon on the wall. This is to honour Priest Vallon as a great warrior.

Voice-Over: Amsterdam Vallon talks through a lot of the film, mainly to give background information about the people of the Five Points. So, it is a lot like *GoodFellas* and *Casino*.

Moral: Priest Vallon: "The blood stays on the blade."

Seeing: Looking through Scorsese's films, *Kundun* was the first that really made the place, rather than the people, the centre of attention. Even though *Casino* takes place in a very defined and confined place, we are still looking at the people and what they are doing in this place. With *Kundun*, Scorsese detached the camera, relaxed and looked around. Similarly, in *Gangs Of New York*, it is the place that is the centre of attention. It is the story of New York told in allegory through the characters. (Perhaps the 'confusion' I feel about *Bringing Out The Dead* probably emanates from Scorsese being caught between a story about the place, and a story about an ambulance driver.) In literary terms, he moved from the first person to the third person. Scorsese has moved into John Ford country, committing his ideas about the world to the screen. He is stating what he thinks about the world.

Having established his environment, Scorsese always keeps the environment in the frame so that the characters interact with their world. The irony of this approach, in this film, is that Bill and Amsterdam don't realise that they have become anachronisms over the course of the film. Paradise Square is the centre of their world but it is not the centre of the world anymore. Their fight at the end of the film is pointless because America has stopped being tribal and has started the unification process, as represented by the Civil War and the Draft Riots. This unification is happening right under their noses, and we see it in the frame, but they do not. We can see members of the gangs intermix with other gangs. For example, McGloin and other Irishmen of the Dead Rabbits join Bill's Federation of American Natives. There are other examples in the dancing (Irish jig and African beats lead to tap dancing) and the songs. This unification is brought out in the pre-fight sequence at the end of the film when Bill and Amsterdam are saying their prayers. By intercutting them, Scorsese is not only showing the characters as being similar, but also showing the religion to be similar.

And talking of religion, Amsterdam carries a medal of St Michael with him at all times (he goes after Jenny to get it back from her when she filches it). At the beginning of the film his father tells him that St Michael cast Satan out of Paradise. Amsterdam is St Michael, Bill is Satan (there are constant references to Bill as Satan: he enters on a fire engine with an infernal red glow behind him; and his hangout is called Satan's Circus) and the whole story is acted out in Paradise Square. So the film becomes a re-enactment of Amsterdam casting Bill out of Paradise.

However, to get to this ending, Amsterdam first rejects his past and his religion. He throws away the *Bible* when he leaves the reformatory and effectively joins Bill's gang. However, the past is always with him. The Old Brewery, which used to be inhabited by the Irish and other nationalities (literally a fermentation of nationalities and cultures), is turned into a church. Later, after his planned revenge goes wrong, Amsterdam turns to the church for refuge and prays. By going back to his roots, and to the church, he gets the moral and physical strength to do the right thing, as per the ancient laws of combat.

Hearing: The cultural melange of New York is heard through the exotic lexicon the characters recite to each other. This is in constant flow, and flows so fast that some of the characters don't know what the words mean. When McGloin calls Amsterdam a fidlam bens, Amsterdam doesn't know what it means. But if he called him a chiseller, then he knows what that is.

The music is also a mixture of cultures. The music for the pre-fight sequence sounds like Irish pipe and drums but is actually the African bamboo flute and drums of Otha Turner (he's superb in Scorsese's blues documentary 'Feel Like Going Home'). During the Chinese Pagoda sequence Bill asks for real American music, and the band play 'Garry Owen', an Irish song (often heard in John Ford Westerns because it is the song of the Seventh Cavalry).

Background: This film had a long gestation period for Scorsese. It was originally announced in *Variety* in 1977 but it just could not get the right script and/or financing. Eventually, Harvey Weinstein of Miramax had the guts to push it forward and found a lot of money to help Scorsese fulfil his dream. Although it had the biggest budget of Scorsese's career ($97 million), it managed to rake in $190 million worldwide before the release of DVD, video and TV rights, so this is Scorsese's greatest financial success.

Verdict: It is rare to see this sort of epic film-making any more. John Ford did *The Iron Horse*. David Lean did *Lawrence Of Arabia*. Steven Spielberg did *Empire Of The Sun*. And now Scorsese digs himself out of a financial and critical slump with a fantastic film that should allow him to write his own ticket for a few more films. What is great is that Scorsese makes a big film about a big subject, but his characters are revealed to be little. It is almost as though instead of printing the legend (as per Ford's *The Man Who Shot Liberty Valance*), Scorsese has decided to print the truth, revelling in the mythology of New York and then debunking it. 5/5

'Feel Like Going Home' in The Blues (2003)

Cast: Interviews: Corey Harris, Taj Mahal, Otha Turner, Pat Thomas, Sam Carr, Dick Waterman, Ali Farka Toure, Habib Koité, Salif Keita, Toumani Diabate, Featured Performers: Corey Harris, Taj Mahal, Otha Turner, Ali Farka Toure, Habib Koité, Salif Keita, Willie King, Keb' Mo', Archival Performances: Son House, Muddy Waters, John Lee Hooker, Johnny Shines, Lead Belly

Crew: Director: Martin Scorsese, Writer: Peter Guralnick, Producer: Sam Pollard, Cinematographer: Arthur Jafa, Editor: David Tedeschi, 110 mins

Background: Scorsese produced seven films showing the origins and development of the blues, from its African roots, through the Mississippi delta, to Chicago and Detroit, and eventually to the UK. Each film has a personal slant. So, for example, Clint Eastwood looks at the pianists, Mike Figgis examines the UK scene, and Wim Wenders concentrates on three of his favourite performers. Scorsese goes back to the origins of the music by starting on the Niger River in Mali and then making his way up through the Mississippi Delta. You should recognise quite a bit of the music because Scorsese has used a lot of it in his films. Otha Turner, for example, is the source for the Irish-sounding drums in *Gangs Of New York*. As well as the seven DVDs, there are lots and lots of repackaged blues CDs to buy. See http://www.pbs. org/theblues/ for more information about the series.

Lady By The Sea: The Statue of Liberty (2004)

Cast: Martin Scorsese (Narrator)

Crew: Director: Martin Scorsese, Writers: Kent Jones, Martin Scorsese, Producers: Martin Scorsese, Edwin Schlossberg (Associate), Editor: Rachel Reichman

Background: The Statue of Liberty has been closed to the public since 11 September 2001, and various organisations have joined together to raise money to pay for the necessary security measures so that it can be reopened. One of the projects was this documentary about the statue commissioned by American Express and The History Channel, which aired on 14 January 2004. For further information on the Campaign to Re-Open the Statue of Liberty visit www.statueofliberty.org.

The Aviator (2004)

Cast: Leonardo DiCaprio (Howard Hughes), Cate Blanchett (Katharine Hepburn), Kate Beckinsale (Ava Gardner), Gwen Stefani (Jean Harlow), Adam Scott (Johnny Meyer), Kelli Garner (Faith Domergue), Ian Holm (Professor Fitz), Alan Alda (Senator Ralph Owen Brewster), Alec Baldwin (Juan Trippe), Willem Dafoe, Stanley DeSantis (Louis B Mayer), Edward Herrmann (Joseph Breen), Danny Huston (Jack Frye), Jude Law (Errol Flynn), John C Reilly (Noah Dietrich)

Crew: Director: Martin Scorsese, Writer: John Logan, Producers: Sandy Climan, Leonardo DiCaprio, Charles Evans Jr., Graham King, Michael Mann, Music: Howard Shore, Cinematographer: Robert Richardson, Editor: Thelma Schoonmaker, Production Designer: Dante Ferretti

Background: This film shows the early life of Howard Hughes and how he amassed a large fortune using his wits and intelligence, taking us from the 1930 production of *Hell's Angels* to the 1947 test flight of the Blue Spruce. This gives Scorsese the opportunity to show films like *The Front Page* and *Scarface* being made, which I'm sure he relished. The film is due for release November 2004 in the US, in time for Oscar consideration no doubt.

And as for the future, there are old projects to consider, like *Dino*, Scorsese's bioflick of Dean Martin, a Bob Dylan music project and a remake of *The Heart Of The Matter*. Meanwhile, although virtually all his films are available on

DVD and video, more keep emerging. *My Voyage To Italy* is out on Region 1 DVD in July 2004, and a 5-film DVD boxset is released in August 2004. The boxset includes remastered disks of *GoodFellas* and *Mean Streets* as well as *After Hours, Alice Doesn't Live Here Anymore* and *Who's That Knocking At My Door?* All have commentaries by Scorsese and other extras.

And so this book comes to an end. But Scorsese doesn't. That he can maintain such a pace and enthusiasm to such a high standard, even after 40 years of film-making, is a tribute to his personal investment in a notoriously unforgiving and fickle art form.

Reference Materials

Books

I just want to mention that probably the best book on Scorsese so far, the one that actually shows him at work, is *The Scorsese Picture* by David Ehrenstein. It was published in 1992 by Birch Lane Press in America but is not well known, so I urge you to go to ebay and bookfinder and amazon to buy a copy.

Authorship And Context: The Films Of Martin Scorsese 1963-1977 by Leighton Grist, Macmillan, 1996

A Cinema Of Loneliness: Penn, Stone, Kubrick, Scorsese, Spielberg, Altman by Robert Phillip Kolker, Oxford University Press, 1980 (revised 1988). An excellent visual analysis of the selected film-makers.

The Cinema Of Martin Scorsese by Laurence Friedman, Continium, 1997. I enjoyed this analysis of the films.

Easy Riders, Raging Bulls by Peter Biskind, Simon & Shuster, 1998. A book that concentrates on the sex and drugs and backstabbing of the 1970s generation of film-makers. Includes much personal material on Scorsese that may or may not be true, or accurate.

Hollywood Rennaissance: Altman, Cassavetes, Coppola, Mazursky, Scorsese And Others by Diane Jacobs, AS Barnes, 1977

Italian And Irish Filmmakers In America: Ford, Capra, Coppola And Scorsese by Lee Lourdeaux, Temple University Press, 1990

Martin Scorsese by Bella Taylor, Scarecrow Press, 1981

Martin Scorsese: A Guide To References And Resources by Marion Weiss, GK Hall, 1987

Martin Scorsese: A Journey by Mary Pat Kelly, Secker & Warburg, 1992. A verbal history of Scorsese the film-maker using new, extensive interviews with the main parties involved. A few people seem to be in there for political reasons and to kiss ass, but the majority is very informative. An updated edition is badly needed, I think.

Martin Scorsese And Michael Cimino by Michael Bliss, Scarecrow Press, 1985

Martin Scorsese: The First Decade by Mary Pat Kelly, Redgrave, 1980

Martin Scorsese Interviews ed Peter Brunette, University of Mississippi, 1999. An excellent collection of interviews, up to *Kundun*.

The Movie Brats by Michael Pye & Lynda Myles, Holt, Rinehart & Winston, 1979. Has sections on each of the film school film-makers to break through in the mid- to late-1970s, including Scorsese.

A Personal Journey With Martin Scorsese Through American Movies by Martin Scorsese, Faber & Faber, 1997. The script of the documentary is published with many stills to illustrate the films mentioned.

Perspectives On Raging Bull ed Steven G Kellman, GK Hall, 1994

Postmodern Auteurs: Coppola, Lucas, De Palma, Spielberg And Scorsese by Kenneth Von Gunden, 1991

Projections 7, ed John Boorman and Walter Donohoe, Faber & Faber, 1997. Contains over 100 pages of text originally edited and written by Scorsese for *Cahiers Du Cinéma*. A big section on *Casino*.

The Scorsese Connection by Lesley Stern, BFI, 1995. An impressionistic journey explaining Scorsese's films in terms of his influences, linking themes and images.

Scorsese On Scorsese, ed David Thompson & Ian Christie, Faber & Faber, 1989 (Revised 1996, 2003). Combines many Scorsese interviews into a comprehensive history.

The Word Made Flesh: Catholicism And Conflict In The Films Of Martin Scorsese by Michael Bliss, Scarecrow Press, 1995

Documentaries

Celebrity Profile: Martin Scorsese (1997) 40 mins – Slick American docu examining life up to *Kundun* including interviews with Scorsese, De Niro, Keitel and many major collaborators.

Scene By Scene With Martin Scorsese (1998) 50 mins – Mark Cousins interviews a relaxed Scorsese using clips with a major section on *Kundun*.

Websites

Scorsese and his films – http://www.scorsesefilms.com/ – News and links to articles.

Martin Scorsese Information Page – http://members.cox.net/scorseseinfo/ – Lots of links to articles and interviews.

De Niro Scorsese – http://www.deniroscorsese.com/ – As the name suggests, a tribute site to both creators, including lots of photos.

Pocket Essentials Stock List

1903047773	Agatha Christie Mark Campbell	3.99
1903047706	Alan Moore Lance Parkin	3.99
1903047528	Alchemy & Alchemists Sean Martin	3.99
1903047005	Alfred Hitchcock NE Paul Duncan	4.99
1903047722	American Civil War Phil Davies	3.99
1903047730	American Indian Wars Howard Hughes	3.99
1903047463	Animation Mark Whitehead	4.99
1903047757	Ancient Greece Mike Paine	3.99
1903047714	Ang Lee Ellen Cheshire	3.99
1903047676	Audrey Hepburn Ellen Cheshire	3.99
190304779X	The Beastie Boys Richard Luck	3.99
1904048196	The Beatles Paul Charles	3.99
1903047854	The Beat Generation Jamie Russell	3.99
1903047366	Billy Wilder Glenn Hopp	3.99
1903047919	Bisexuality Angie Bowie	3.99
1903047749	Black Death Sean Martin	3.99
1903047587	Blaxploitation Films Mikel J Koven	3.99
1904048307	Bohemian London Travis Elborough 9.99hb (Oct 2004)	
1903047455	Bollywood Ashok Banker	3.99
1903047129	Brian de Palma John Ashbrook	3.99
1903047579	Bruce Lee Simon B Kenny	3.99
1904048331	The Cathars Sean Martin	
190404803X	Carry On Films Mark Campbell	3.99
1904048048	Classic Radio Comedy Nat Coward	3.99
1903047811	Clint Eastwood Michael Carlson	3.99
1903047307	Conspiracy Theories Robin Ramsay	3.99
1904048099	Creative Writing Neil Nixon	3.99
1903047536	The Crusades Mike Paine	3.99
1903047285	Cyberpunk Andrew M Butler	3.99
1903047269	David Cronenberg John Costello	3.99
1903047064	David Lynch Le Blanc/Odell	3.99
1903047196	Doctor Who Mark Campbell	3.99
1904048277	Do Your Own PR Richard Milton	3.99
190304751X	Feminism Susan Osborne	3.99
1903047633	Film Music Paul Tonks	3.99
1903047080	Film Noir Paul Duncan	3.99
1904048080	Film Studies Andrew M Butler	3.99
190304748X	Filming on a Microbudget NE Paul Hardy 4.99 (July 2004)	

190304765X	French New Wave Chris Wiegand	3.99
1903047544	Freud & Psychoanalysis Nick Rennison	3.99
1904048218	Georges Simenon David Carter	3.99
1903047943	George Lucas James Clarke	3.99
1904048013	German Expressionist Films Paul Cooke	3.99
1904048161	Globalisation Steven P McGiffen	3.99
1904048145	Hal Hartley Jason Wood	3.99
1904048110	Hammer Films John McCarty	3.99
1903047994	History of Witchcraft Lois Martin	3.99
1903047404	Hitchhiker's Guide M J Simpson	3.99
1903047072	Hong Kong's Heroic Bloodshed Martin Fitzgerald	3.99
1903047382	Horror Films Le Blanc/Odell	3.99
1903047692	Jack the Ripper Whitehead/Rivett	3.99
1903047102	Jackie Chan Le Blanc/Odell	3.99
1903047951	James Cameron Brian J Robb	3.99
1903047242	Jane Campion Ellen Cheshire	3.99
1904048188	Jethro Tull Raymond Benson	3.99
1904048331	Joel & Ethan Coen Cheshire/Ashbrook NE 4.99 (Nov 04)	
1903047374	John Carpenter Le Blanc/Odell	3.99
1904048285	The Knights Templar Sean Martin 9.99 HB	
1903047250	Krzystzof Kieslowski Monika Maurer	3.99
1903047609	Laurel & Hardy Brian J Robb	3.99
1903047803	The Madchester Scene Richard Luck	3.99
1903047315	Marilyn Monroe Paul Donnelley	3.99
1903047668	Martin Scorsese Paul Duncan 4.99 (Jul 2004)	
1903047595	The Marx Brothers Mark Bego	3.99
1903047846	Michael Mann Mark Steensland	3.99
1903047641	Mike Hodges Mark Adams	3.99
1903047498	Nietzsche Travis Elborough	3.99
1903047110	Noir Fiction Paul Duncan	3.99
1904048226	Nuclear Paranoia C Newkey-Burden	3.99
1903047927	Oliver Stone Michael Carlson	3.99
1903047048	Orson Welles Martin Fitzgerald	3.99
1903047293	Philip K Dick Andrew M Butler	3.99
1904048242	Postmodernism Andrew M Butler	3.99
1903047560	Ridley Scott Brian Robb	3.99
1903047838	The Rise of New Labour Robin Ramsay	3.99
1904048102	Roger Corman Mark Whitehead	3.99

1903047897	Roman Polanski Daniel Bird 3.99
1903047447	Science Fiction Films John Costello 4.99 (Oct 04)
1903047412	Sergio Leone Michael Carlson 3.99
1903047684	Sherlock Holmes Mark Campbell 3.99
1903047277	Slasher Movies Mark Whitehead 3.99
1904048072	Spike Lee Darren Arnold 3.99
1903047013	Stanley Kubrick Paul Duncan 3.99
190304782X	Steven Soderbergh Jason Wood 3.99
1903047439	Steven Spielberg James Clarke 4.99
1903047331	Stock Market Essentials Victor Cuadra 3.99
1904048064	Succeed in Music Business Paul Charles 3.99
1903047765	Successful Sports Agent Mel Stein 3.99
1904048366	Tarantino D K Holm 4.99 (Nov 2004)
1903047145	Terry Gilliam John Ashbrook 3.99
1903047390	Terry Pratchett Andrew M Butler 3.99
1903047625	Tim Burton Le Blanc/Odell 3.99
190404817X	Tintin J M & R Lofficier 3.99
1903047889	UFOs Neil Nixon 3.99
1904048250	The Universe Richard Osborne 9.99 (HB)
190304717X	Vampire Films Le Blanc/Odell 3.99
190404820X	Videogaming Flatley & French 3.99
1903047935	Vietnam War Movies Jamie Russell 3.99
1904048129	Who Shot JFK? Robin Ramsay 3.99
1904048056	William Shakespeare Ian Nichols 3.99
1903047056	Woody Allen Martin Fitzgerald 3.99
1903047471	Writing a Screenplay John Costello 4.99

Available from all good bookshops or send a cheque to:
Pocket Essentials P.O. Box 394, Harpenden, Herts, AL5 1XJ.
Please make cheques payable to **'Oldcastle Books'**, add 50p for
postage and packing for each book in the UK and £1 elsewhere.

Customers worldwide can order online at
www.pocketessentials.com